The Divine Substitute

The atonement in the Bible and history

© Day One Publications 2006
First printed 2006

ISBN 1 84625 038 -2

9 781846 250385

Unless otherwise stated, all Scripture quotations are from the
New International Version copyright © 1973, 1978, 1984

British Library Cataloguing in Publication Data available

Published by Day One Publications
Ryelands Road, Leominster, HR6 8NZ
☎ 01568 613 740 FAX 01568 611 473
email—sales@dayone.co.uk
web site—www.dayone.co.uk
North American—e-mail—sales@dayonebookstore.com
North American—web site—www.dayonebookstore.com

Designed by Steve Devane and printed by Gutenberg Press, Malta

Contents

Acknowledgements

Particular thanks are due to Dr Garry Williams, Dr Geoffrey Grogan, Dr Graham Keith, and Rev. Eryl Rowlands who have kindly given of their time to comment on all, or parts, of the text of this book. Their input has proved most valuable. Thanks are also due to International Christian College, Glasgow, for granting flexibility in a busy workload schedule to enable Dr Ian Shaw to undertake his contribution to this book.

John Wesley once claimed that nothing in Christian teaching 'is of greater importance than the doctrine of the atonement.'[1] This book is based on the conviction that Wesley was right. It begins with a statement of the biblical doctrine of the atonement followed by a survey of the broad Christian tradition from the early church to the present day. The deliberate focus is upon one specific aspect of the atonement: that of Christ's death as a divine substitute for sinners.

In days when immediacy is everything, and when instant solutions are demanded, there is a great danger that in an effort to appear contemporary, Christians in the present generation will lose sight of the rich heritage of church teaching in this area. Rediscovering this tradition helps to counter views, both from within and outside the church, that would destabilise the faith of Christians and lead unsuspecting believers down routes that could prove spiritually harmful. Viewing the issue of Christ bearing the punishment in the place of sinners, through the lens of Christian history, helps us to appreciate why the church has come to understand the teaching of the Bible in a certain way, and why some approaches have been rejected in the past, and others retained. It raises fundamental questions about new developments—why has this not been adopted by the Christian church before? Many modern views of the atonement are a reworking of long rejected ideas, simply presented in contemporary packaging.

The richness of the way in which the Bible refers to the work of Christ upon the cross has been reflected in Christian writings throughout the history of the church. However, at the heart of Biblical teaching about the atonement is the substitutionary death of Jesus Christ, bearing the just penalty for sins. This profound truth draws together all other ways of speaking about the atonement; it is the operative principle that lies behind them. What this book shows is that this teaching on the penal and substitutionary death of Christ is not simply the product of one particular time or context. Although distinctive contributions have been made in certain eras, it is a glorious theme that has been taught at every period in the history of the church.

---

1 **J. Wesley,** *Letters of John Wesley*, ed. J. Telford, Vol 6 (London: Epworth Press, 1931) p. 297.

Variations from this perspective have, until comparatively recently, been rejected as erroneous and dangerous, and have often been associated with error in other areas—such as holding liberal views of the Trinity or Scripture. Contemporary Christians should be not only biblically literate about these issues, but also historically literate. This is why the historical section of the book is also important. This survey is only representative, and far from exhaustive. Hopefully it will encourage further study, reflection, and a challenge to believe—and lovingly proclaim—these truths with renewed courage and faithfulness.

J ust along the coast from Edinburgh by the Firth of Forth, is the village of Prestonpans. It was here in September 1745 that the forces of the English Parliament suffered a serious defeat at the hands of the forces of Bonny Prince Charlie. A senior officer in command of the English troops was killed in that battle—his name was Colonel James Gardiner.

Gardiner was born in 1688, the year that King William arrived from Holland to take the throne of England. Gardiner's father died fighting for the king in Germany and, though his mother was a fine Christian, James grew up to be wild and reckless. He fought his first duel at the age of eight, for which he bore a scar for life, and at fourteen was an ensign in a Scottish regiment fighting in Holland. Five years later he was present at the Battle of Ramilles in the War of the Spanish Succession. It is said that in combat he fought like a man possessed and in this battle Gardiner rushed forward with the colours, uttering oaths and curses that made his comrades wince. A musket ball entered his mouth and came out of his neck within an inch of his vertebrae. He lay on the field all night and only by a miracle he survived.

From the age of nineteen to thirty Gardiner was, in his own words, 'wild, thoughtless and wretched.' Eventually he was assigned to diplomatic service, and in the French court he was known as 'a happy rake'. But he was not happy and claimed that at times he even envied a dog.

In July 1719, at the age of thirty-two, Gardiner had spent a Sunday evening in cheap entertainment, and planned a midnight meeting with a married woman. At 11 o'clock he was waiting for his liaison and idly turned the pages of *The Christian Soldier or Heaven Taken by Storm* by the Puritan Thomas Watson. Suddenly he saw a blaze of light and had a vision of the cross; he heard the words: 'O sinner! Did I suffer this for thee, and are these the returns?'

For three months Gardiner was under a terrible conviction of sin, knowing himself to be worthy of hell and seeing himself as a monster in the light of Calvary. Then, one day in October 1719, James Gardiner read, in the King James Authorized Version, the words of the apostle Paul in Romans 3:25–26 explaining the significance of the death of Christ:

'Whom God hath set forth *to be* a propitiation through faith in his blood, to declare his righteousness for the remission of sins that are past, through the forbearance of God; to declare, *I say*, at this time his righteousness: that he might be just, and the justifier of him which believeth in Jesus.'

Immediately his life was transformed. Gardiner became an excellent officer and would spend two hours with God every morning, however early the army had to be on the move. By June 1743 he was in command of a regiment of dragoons and wrote home to his wife: 'Let me die wherever it shall please God, or whenever it shall be. I am sure I shall go to the mansions of eternal glory and enjoy my God and my Redeemer in heaven for ever.' That day came on Saturday 21 September 1745 on the field of the disastrous defeat of the English at Prestonpans.[1]

What was so powerful about those verses that they transformed the life of this tough soldier? What is it about these verses that has proved a source of such confidence and comfort to generations of Christians before and after? The view of Christ's death found in that passage in Romans 3 is the particular focus of this book, considered from both biblical and historical perspectives.

---

1 **Philip Doddridge,** *The Life of Colonel James Gardiner* (Allman and Sons, n.d.).

PART ONE

The biblical record

If you were asked, 'What lies at the very heart of the Christian gospel?' how would you reply? To the apostle Paul, 'of first importance' was that 'Christ died for our sins according to the Scriptures' (1 Corinthians 15:3). That is one of the most outstanding statements of the Christian faith. Paul was convinced that the cross was for 'our sins', and that it fulfilled Old Testament Scripture. He sets the death of Christ at the heart of the whole message of the Bible. Through the cross sin is dealt with, the way of reconciliation with God is established, atonement is made. However, this poses two vital questions that must be answered before we can understand the way of atonement: Why is atonement needed, and what is the nature of the God who planned it? To have a proper view of the atonement we must start with a proper view of sin, and how it is viewed by a just and holy God. If we err here, the consequences will be profound.

First, why is atonement needed?

All is not well with the world because all is not well with its inhabitants. There is certainly much beauty and love, enjoyment and compassion, to be found in this world. But there is also ugliness and cruelty, misery and pain. Where have these come from? The Bible explains in Genesis 3 how the world, created perfect by God, was spoilt in every part by an act of disobedience that left humanity out of step with God. Tragic consequences followed this 'Fall'.

REBELLION AGAINST GOD

One way the Bible defines sin is rebellion against God. In Psalm 51:1 the word 'transgressions' is *peshah*, or rebellion. Sin is disobeying God's commands, distrusting his words and rejecting his authority. Through rebellion the human race lost touch with God, and man-made religions were fashioned: 'Their thinking became futile and their foolish hearts were darkened. Although they claimed to be wise, they became fools and exchanged the glory of the immortal God for images made to look like mortal man and birds and animals and reptiles' (Romans 1:21–22, see also 1 Corinthians 2:14). The Creator was rejected and ignorance ruled, even though God's 'invisible qualities' were evident in creation (Romans 1:20). Throughout history God compassionately gave laws that would limit the excesses of rebellion, but the human race has consistently ignored them.

REBELLION BROUGHT SLAVERY

The Fall has locked the human race into the slavery of sin. For all its religious activity, humanity cannot clear itself of sin. It has been well expressed in the phrase: 'man is free to sin but not free not to sin.' It is not that men and women can never do right, but they cannot do right all the time. They are not as bad as they could be, but no one is as good as they should be. The Fall into sin brought the human race into slavery to the author of sin—Satan; Paul described him as 'the spirit who is now at work in those who are disobedient' (Ephesians 2:2).

What the Bible says about this cannot be ignored. Paul told the Christians at Rome that they 'used to be slaves to sin' and that they were 'slaves to the one' whom they obeyed (Romans 5:16–17), and he informed those at Corinth that Satan is the 'god of this age' who has 'blinded the minds of unbelievers' (2 Corinthians 4:4). Peter agreed: 'A man is a slave to whatever has mastered him' (2 Peter 2:19). And so wrote the apostle John: 'He who does what is sinful is of the devil' (1 John 3:8). Jesus himself was equally clear on this point: 'I tell you the truth, everyone who sins is a slave to sin.' (John 8:34). This is clearly a biblical theme.

In the light of assertions by many that the human race is inherently good rather than inherently sinful, the implications of the words of Jesus should not be ignored: 'If you, then, though you are evil, know how to give good gifts to your children ...' (Matthew 7:11): Jesus concluded that we are evil but sometimes do good, rather than saying we are good but sometimes do evil.

REBELLION BROUGHT DEATH

The first rebellion brought spiritual and physical death (Genesis 2:17). Humanity was left dead in 'transgressions and sins' (Ephesians 2:1), that is, cut off from contact with God or a desire for him. Physical death followed; as the Puritan, Thomas Watson expressed it: 'sin dug Adam's grave.'[1] The consequences still reverberate through the human race: 'Therefore ... sin entered the world through one man, and death through sin, and in this way death came to all men, because all sinned (Romans 5:12). Death became the enemy that stalks our path.

It was not only the human race that was damaged by the Fall. So too was the natural creation: 'The whole creation has been groaning, as in the pain of childbirth, right up to the present time' (Romans 8:22). The harmony of creation was upset and nature became 'red in tooth and claw'; from hurricanes to tsunamis, natural disasters began to wreak havoc on the earth.

REBELLION BROUGHT JUDGEMENT

Because God is holy and just, ultimately the human race must be held accountable to him for their rebellion. Sin may not always receive its just deserts in this life, but there is a day of reckoning for everyone: 'Man is destined to die once, and after that to face Judgement' (Hebrews 9:27). At this judgement there will be no defence: 'The whole world [will be] held accountable to God' (Romans 3:19).

Some have denied this. The New Testament scholar, C.H. Dodd, claimed that 'wrath' does not describe God's attitude to the human race but only the 'inevitable process of cause and effect in a moral universe.'[2] Certainly Paul did speak of God's wrath in the present tense, but it is clearly God's wrath revealed from heaven against the wickedness of men (Romans 1:18), not merely some 'inevitable process of cause and effect.' There is far too much evidence in the New Testament to doubt that wrath has a fearful future perspective. Paul wrote:

---

1 **Thomas Watson,** *A Body of Divinity* (London: 1692, republished London: Banner of Truth, 1958), Q. XIX 3rd misery, p. 152.

2 **C.H. Dodd,** *The Epistle to the Romans* (London: Hodder and Stoughton, 1932), p. 23.

This will happen when the Lord Jesus is revealed from heaven in blazing fire with his powerful angels. He will punish those who do not know God and do not obey the gospel of our Lord Jesus. They will be punished with everlasting destruction and shut out from the presence of the Lord and from the majesty of his power (2 Thessalonians 1:7–9).

And further:

For those who are self-seeking and who reject the truth and follow evil, there will be wrath and anger (Romans 2:8).

Jesus himself addressed the same theme:

The Son of Man will send out his angels, and they will weed out of his kingdom everything that causes sin and all who do evil. They will throw them into the fiery furnace, where there will be weeping and gnashing of teeth. Then the righteous will shine like the sun in the kingdom of their Father (Matthew 13:41–43).

According to the apostle Peter the heavens and the earth are 'being kept for the day of judgement and destruction of ungodly men' (2 Peter 3:7). The writer to the Hebrews warned that it will be 'a fearful expectation of judgement and of raging fire that will consume the enemies of God' (Hebrews 10:27).

No one pretends that this is a pleasant picture, but unless we are prepared to deny that such passages have any relevance whatever, we must accept the reality of a final, unavoidable day of accountability to God.

In summary, sin is falling short of God's perfect standards; God is holy, and therefore the rebellion of sin is an offence in his sight. God is also absolutely just, and he must punish sin. There are fearful consequences for those who die with their sin unforgiven.

This diagnosis of the human race has probably never been as out of favour as it is today; some professing Christians would prefer to deny it rather than challenge the viewpoint of our optimistic world. Yet, to deny these facts is to deny the authority of Scripture. As we said at the start, to have a proper view of the atonement we must begin with a proper view of sin, and how it is viewed by a just and holy God. If we err here, the consequences will be profound.

Second, what is the nature of God?

To understand the tragic consequences of the Fall for the human race is only half way to appreciating the way of the atonement. We must also understand something of the nature of God. What kind of God is he? No description can exhaust the qualities of the omnipotent Creator God, and it is almost presumptuous to try, but for our subject, we can establish four facts about God that were clearly taught in the Hebrew Scriptures and underlined by Jesus and the apostles: God is holy, God hates sin, God is just and must punish sin, God is merciful.

GOD IS SUPREMELY HOLY

It is one of the great errors of our modern age, and into which too many well-meaning Christians fall, that one of the attributes of God is singled out and placed above all others. It is almost always the attribute of love that is given pride of place. It has been claimed that love is the most important quality that we attribute to God, it is 'the first and last word in the biblical portrait' of God[3] and that, as a consequence 'The Bible never defines God as anger, power or judgement—in fact it never defines him as anything other than love.'[4] This is simply not true. The Bible describes the character of God in a multitude of ways. He is 'a consuming fire'(Deuteronomy 4:24), 'a righteous judge (Psalm 7:11), 'righteous' (Daniel 9:14), 'truthful'(John 3:33), 'just' (2 Thessalonians 1:6), 'living and active' (Hebrews 4:12) 'light' (1 John 1:5), 'holy' (Psalm 99:9), 'merciful' (Deuteronomy 4:31), 'gracious and compassionate' (2 Chronicles 30:9)— and much more besides.

To elevate one aspect of God above all others is both unbalanced and dangerous. Unlike us, who can be sometimes one thing and sometimes another, God is all that he is all the time; he is never one thing or another, he

---

3   **C. Pinnock, ed.,** The Openness of God. (Carlisle: Paternoster, 1994), p. 18.

4   **S. Chalke and A. Mann,** The Lost Message of Jesus (London: Zondervan, 2003), p. 63.

is always everything that he is. He described himself in this way: 'I the Lord do not change' (Malachi 3:6), and James referred to him as the 'Father of the heavenly lights, who does not change like shifting shadows' (James 1:17). It is true that there are times when his love and mercy are seen most clearly, and other times when his anger and justice come to the fore, but when he is revealed as a God of judgement, he does not cease to be a God of love, and when he is seen in overwhelming mercy and compassion, he does not cease to be a Creator who is absolutely holy and pure and who insists on implicit obedience to his commands and who threatens serious consequences to those who defy him. This cannot be emphasised too much. Many false theologies today stem from this basic misunderstanding by allowing one characteristic of God to usurp all others. Thus, to declare the awesome holiness of God and his implacable hatred of sin in all its forms, does not in any way deny the overwhelming mercy and compassion of that same God.

When Moses was told that he could not see the face of God, 'for no-one may see me and live' (Exodus 33:20), it was not, as one has suggested, because the face of God was etched with all the suffering that has ever taken place,[5] but because God's holiness was too brilliantly pure for any man to see him as he is. That this is the only proper understanding of that prohibition 'no-one may see me and live', is clear from the fact that whenever Moses met with God in the Tabernacle, a veil had to be put over his face when he came out to the people because 'they saw that his face was radiant' (Exodus 34:29–35). This is not a reflection of pain and suffering in the face of God, but of purity and holiness; a point that is made clear by Paul in 2 Corinthians 3:7, 'the Israelites could not look steadily at the face of Moses because of its glory …'. Here the word glory (*doxa*) refers to the full character of God and is the equivalent of the Hebrew word *kabowd*, used frequently in the Old Testament to describe the presence of God (see Exodus 33:18–22 for example). It is because God 'lives in unapproachable light' (1 Timothy 6:16), that we cannot see him—not because he lives in unapproachable pain and suffering.

---

5 **Chalke and Mann,** *The Lost Message of Jesus,* pp. 58–59.

As a result of his own holiness, God expected his people to be holy also. And his standard was very high: 'Be holy because I am holy' (Leviticus 11:44–45) was the order of the day and every day. The phrase 'be holy' occurs frequently in the Hebrew Scriptures and it covered every part of the life of the nation. It was linked with their food laws, health and hygiene, their tithe offerings to God, the clothes they wore, even the cleanliness of the camp; everything was carefully regulated because they must 'be holy'. In fact, the righteousness of his laws, unique in the ancient world, would itself be a testimony of the righteousness of God to the surrounding nations (Deuteronomy 4:6–8).

GOD HATES SIN IN ALL ITS FORMS

If God is supremely holy, we might expect it to follow that he hates sin because it defies his authority, defiles his creation and his moral nature reacts against it. Throughout the Old Testament God underlined the gravity of sin and his relentless opposition to it. The word that is most commonly employed to describe God's response to sin is the Hebrew *towebah*. The older translations render it by 'abomination', and it is a strong word for something disgusting, loathsome or detestable—and 'detestable' is how the New International Version translates it, where it appears some 117 times in the Old Testament.

This is how much God detests even 'commonplace' sins:

There are six things the Lord hates, seven that are detestable to him: haughty eyes, a lying tongue, hands that shed innocent blood, a heart that devises wicked schemes, feet that are quick to rush into evil, a false witness who pours out lies and a man who stirs up dissension among brothers (Proverbs 6:16–18).

His hatred of the disgusting ways of the godless nations that Israel had adopted during their Babylonian exile is graphically stated in Ezekiel 7:8–9:

I am about to pour out my wrath on you and spend my anger against you; I will judge you according to your conduct and repay you for all your detestable practices. I will not look on you with pity or spare you; I will repay you in accordance with your conduct and the detestable practices among you. Then you will know that it is I the Lord who strikes the blow.

And again:

'Do not plot evil against your neighbour, and do not love to swear falsely. I hate all this,' declares the Lord (Zechariah 8:17).

There is perhaps no more powerful word in the Hebrew that could express strong abhorrence for something. Whilst it is chiefly used of God, it is not exclusively so: the same word is used to describe the cultural and ritual contamination of an Egyptian eating with the Hebrews (Genesis 43:32). However, when used of God, a wide range of practices fall under *towebah*, from homosexual behaviour and other perversions (Leviticus 18:22–30), idolatry (Deuteronomy 7:25), human sacrifice (Deuteronomy 12:31), and dishonest dealing (Deuteronomy 25:13–16). The word became a synonym for an idol as 'a detestable thing' (Isaiah 44:19).

The opposition of God to all kinds of sin, meant that he even taught his people to recognise the existence of sins committed in ignorance as well as those wilfully committed. These unintentional sins were not overlooked as if they did not matter—in the same way that in our modern society, ignorance of the law is no excuse for breaking it. There were special sacrifices that had to be offered for these unintentional sins (see Numbers 15:22–29).

However, this was no quirk peculiar to the old covenant period. It is too often assumed that the anger of God is entirely absent in the teaching of Jesus and Paul. The two common words in Greek that express anger are *thumos* and *orge*. The first implies being hot with emotion, breathing

---

6 For the distinction see the Greek Lexicon of **Grimm/Thayer** (Edinburgh: T&T Clark, 1892). Also **Arndt & Gingrich (Bauer)** (University of Chicago Press,1979) and **W.E. Vine,** *The Expository Dictionary of New Testament Words* (London: Oliphants, 1964). Some recent scholarship sees less distinction between the words, but see **G. Kittel and G. Friedrich,** *Theological Dictionary of the New Testament,* (Abridged in one volume by **G.W. Bromiley**) (Grand Rapids: Eerdmans, 1985), p. 722, where a distinction in NT usage is noted.

violence; apart from Revelation this word is used only once of God in the New Testament. The second word refers to a strong, but steady and settled anger; and this is the word used for God's anger. The one boils up and subsides whilst the other arises gradually and is settled.[6] In Romans 2:8 both words are used with reference to the response of God to sin: 'For those who are self-seeking and who reject the truth and follow evil, there will be wrath (*orge*) and anger (*thumos*).' The only other place where they are coupled is Revelation 16:19 where 'the fury (*thumos*) of his wrath (*orge*)' vividly expresses the final judgement of God upon 'Babylon'.

Once Jesus is recorded as being wrathful (*orge*) in Mark 3:5 (though the NIV translates the word by 'anger'). Undeniably he saw the ultimate judgement of the unbelieving as an expression of divine wrath: 'Whoever rejects the Son will not see life, for God's wrath remains on him' (John 3:36). In Romans 1:18–32, Paul did not spare his readers with his explicit description of the sinfulness of the entire human race and the consequence that since no one is righteous, everyone is under the 'wrath of God' which 'is being revealed from heaven' (1:18). In Ephesians 2:3 the same apostle concluded that universal sin means that all are 'by nature objects of wrath', and in Ephesians 5:6 and Colossians 3:6 this same wrath is both present and future. Salvation is not less than being saved 'from God's wrath' (Romans 5:9).

It may be currently unpopular to write and speak of the wrath of God, but this theme is stamped indelibly on the pages of Scripture. Leon Morris concluded that there are more than twenty words that refer to the anger of God in the Old Testament, and they are used a total of 580 times.[7] However, this anger is not capricious; it is the result of human sin. Nor is God's mercy a trade-off for human goodness, rather it is the wholly unmerited kindness of God. Since both anger and love are expressed, we must understand them as two compatible aspects of the divine nature.

GOD IS JUST AND MUST PUNISH SIN

It is an inescapable fact that throughout the Old Testament there is a

---

7 **L. Morris,** *The Apostolic Preaching of the Cross* (London: Tyndale Press, 1960), p. 131.

constant reminder that God is just and that sin carries serious consequences, and these come in two forms. First, there is the natural result of sin—to break God's laws will inevitably spoil lives. But there is also a spiritual result of sin—the nation and the individual are answerable to God. However much God loved his chosen people Israel, he would not spare them if they failed to obey his laws; and it is no light warning that he gave:

> But if you will not listen to me and carry out all these commands, and if you reject my decrees and abhor my laws and fail to carry out all my commands and so violate my covenant, then I will do this to you: I will bring upon you sudden terror, wasting diseases and fever that will destroy your sight and drain away your life. You will plant seed in vain, because your enemies will eat it. I will set my face against you so that you will be defeated by your enemies; those who hate you will rule over you, and you will flee even when no-one is pursuing you. If after all this you will not listen to me, I will punish you for your sins seven times over. I will break down your stubborn pride and make the sky above you like iron and the ground beneath you like bronze (Leviticus 26:14–19).

Everything would be against them: health, wealth and neighbours.

Just before the end of his life, Moses warned the people that they had before them the choice of obedience or disobedience and the result of their choice would be either a blessing or curse:

> I command you today to love the Lord your God, to walk in his ways, and to keep his commands, decrees and laws; then you will live and increase, and the Lord your God will bless you in the land you are entering to possess. But if your heart turns away and you are not obedient, and if you are drawn away to bow down to other gods and worship them, I declare to you this day that you will certainly be destroyed. You will not live long in the land you are crossing the Jordan to enter and possess. This day I call heaven and earth as witnesses against you that I have set before you life and death, blessings and curses (Deuteronomy 30:16–19).

To underline this, when the Israelites entered their promised land, half the Levites ascended Mount Gerizim where they recited the blessings that would follow obedience to the law of God, whilst the other half ascended

Mount Ebal to warn of the curses that would follow disobedience (Deuteronomy 27–28).

None of this is limited to the Old Testament, as if God had somehow become more accustomed to sin, or more tolerant of it, as the centuries passed. Jesus was unambiguous on this subject. C.S. Lewis insisted that the doctrine of hell, 'Has the full support of Scripture and, specially, of our Lord's own words.'[8] Indeed, all the most horrifying texts come from the mouth of our Lord; they include: 'hell', 'the fire of hell', 'condemned to hell', 'eternal condemnation', 'the resurrection of condemnation', 'eternal fire', 'outer darkness', 'the place of torment', 'the road that leads to destruction', 'hell, where their worm does not die and the fire is not quenched', 'the place of weeping and gnashing of teeth', 'eternal punishment'. If these phrases prove nothing else, they must surely demonstrate that the Son of God shared his Father's hatred of sin and the ultimate determination to punish the unrepentant sinner. If this is not so, then words have lost all meaning. C.S. Lewis made the telling point that 'our Lord often speaks of hell as a sentence inflicted by a tribunal'[9] and referred to John 12:48 as one example:

There is a judge for the one who rejects me and does not accept my words; that very word which I spoke will condemn him at the last day.

Paul did not spare the human race in his condemnation of sin either: 'The wrath of God is being revealed from heaven against all the godlessness and wickedness of men who suppress the truth by their wickedness' (Romans 1:18). Neither did he spare those in the church who played fast and loose with holy things:

A man ought to examine himself before he eats of the bread and drinks of the cup. For anyone who eats and drinks without recognising the body of the Lord eats and drinks Judgement on himself. That is why many among you are weak and sick, and a number

---

8 C.S. Lewis, *The Problem of Pain* (London: The Centenary Press. 1940), p. 106.

9 Lewis, *The Problem of Pain,* p. 111.

of you have fallen asleep. But if we judged ourselves, we would not come under Judgement. When we are judged by the Lord, we are being disciplined so that we will not be condemned with the world (1 Corinthians 11:28–32).

James similarly warned his readers of the danger of tolerating sin and urged them:

Come near to God and he will come near to you. Wash your hands, you sinners, and purify your hearts, you double-minded. Grieve, mourn and wail. Change your laughter to mourning and your joy to gloom. Humble yourselves before the Lord, and he will lift you up (James 4:8–10).

Likewise Jude was strident in his denunciation of sin and warned those in the church who were leading others into error, of the punishment of Sodom and Gomorrah (Jude 4–7).

The whole of the Bible is insistent that all men and women are accountable to God, and that there is a day of reckoning approaching when:

He will pay back trouble to those who trouble you ... He will punish those who do not know God and do not obey the gospel of our Lord Jesus. They will be punished with everlasting destruction and shut out from the presence of the Lord and from the majesty of his power (2 Thessalonians 1:6–9).

Paul prefaced this solemn warning with the significant phrase 'God is just'.

This was not a vindictive God demanding obedience—or else; rather, it was a serious warning that because God is just, sin always brings dire consequences and obedience is always the best way for people to live. That is how life is. A holy God cannot simply ignore sin without implying that it does not matter, any more than a nation's justice system can turn a blind eye to corruption and crime without compromising its own integrity and that of the laws it is there to uphold. God is not passive in the face of a world full of sin. Three times in Romans 1 Paul reminded his readers that God 'gave them over' (vs 24,26,28) to the result of their own evil. This is not a passive unconcern, but part of his active punishment of rebellion against his laws.

Leon Morris well expressed the true understanding of the anger of God against sin: 'Those who object to the conception of the wrath of God should realise that what is meant is not some irrational passion bursting forth uncontrollably, but a burning zeal for the right coupled with a perfect hatred for everything that is evil.'[10] However, we should never imagine that God's anger against sin is in defence of some law to which he himself is subject, on the contrary, it is from the necessity arising from his own nature as an infinitely holy and just Creator.

GOD IS OUTSTANDINGLY MERCIFUL

The *maskil* of Asaph (Psalm 78) contains one of the most powerful expressions of the way the Israelite viewed the mercy of God. It begins with a tribute to the kindness of God in providing firm laws for each succeeding generation to follow, backed by the gracious actions of the God who provided for his people at every point in their long and colourful history: He did miracles, divided the sea for them to cross over, and split the rocks to provide water. Sadly, and this takes up the larger part of the psalm, the people constantly forgot God and broke his laws—in modern parlance, they threw his love back in his face and thumbed their nose at God. At times 'he was very angry' (v 21) and punished them severely, yet still he 'opened the doors of heaven' and rained down bread for them to eat. Even when they were punished and returned to God in repentance, often their hearts were not loyal and they were 'lying to him with their tongues.' Remarkably, however, God had pity on them, and in a magnificent statement about the character of God that could not be matched in all the writings of pagan literature, Asaph continued:

'Yet he, being compassionate, atoned for their iniquity and did not destroy them. He restrained his anger often, and did not stir up all his wrath. He remembered that they were but flesh, a wind that passes and comes not again' (vs 38–39 ESV).

Here, *Kaphar* is the word correctly translated 'atoned'. But notice that it was God himself who atoned for a rebellious people. When Moses had met with God on Sinai, it was God who described his own character: 'The Lord,

---

10 L. Morris, *The Apostolic Preaching of the Cross.* (London: Tyndale Press, 1960), p. 181.

the Lord, the compassionate and gracious God, slow to anger, abounding in love and faithfulness, maintaining love to thousands, and forgiving wickedness, rebellion and sin. Yet he does not leave the guilty unpunished ...' Exodus 34:6–7.

In a similar vein, and perhaps a few centuries beyond Asaph, the prophet Micah launched into a magnificent paean of praise for the mercy of God:

Who is a God like you, who pardons sin and forgives the transgression of the remnant of his inheritance? You do not stay angry for ever but delight to show mercy. You will again have compassion on us; you will tread our sins underfoot and hurl all our iniquities into the depths of the sea (Micah 7:18–19).

Notice that from Moses to Asaph to Micah—across seven hundred years of Israel's history—the dual character of God is placed side by side: compassion and anger. How to reconcile the severe anger of God against sin, and his willing forgiveness of the sinner is precisely the point at which atonement comes into focus. The entire sacrificial and ceremonial system of the Hebrews, was built around two great principles of the God of Israel: First that God must punish sin, and second that he longs to spare the sinner. The severity of judgement must never be allowed to cloud the free grace of forgiveness for the repentant sinner. Again and again God promised that however disobedient his people had been, if only they would return to him in repentance, there would be free and abundant forgiveness for them.

God adorned his promise of forgiveness with vivid metaphors to convince his people that it is not a mere passing mood or transient warm feeling, but that forgiveness is final, free and for ever. This is how he will treat their sins: He will replace their scarlet sins with the whiteness of snow (Isaiah 1:18), cast them behind his back (Isaiah 38:17), blot them out and never again bring them to mind (Isaiah 43:25), sweep them away like a dissolving cloud or mist (Isaiah 44:22), tread them into the ground without trace and cast them into the depths of the sea (Micah 7:19), and he will

---

11 **Chalke and Mann,** *The Lost Message of Jesus*, p. 109.

remove their transgressions as far as the east is from the west (Psalm 103:8–12).

One contemporary writer has suggested that, 'When it comes to the God of the Bible there is only one kind of sin in the world—forgiven sin'.[11] That is an unbelievable error. The exact opposite is the truth. As far as the God of the Bible is concerned, forgiven sin no longer exists. It is unforgiven sin that remains to be dealt with.

The pictures are no less powerful in the New Testament. Paul told his readers that God has, 'forgiven us all our trespasses, by cancelling the record of debt that stood against us with its legal demands' (Colossians 2:13–14 ESV). The verb 'forgiven' is derived directly from the noun 'grace', and it means 'to show oneself gracious'. The phrase 'the record of debt' translates just one word in the Greek (*cheirographon*), which was commonly used in the first century. It referred to a certificate of debt written with one's own hand—a promise that in due time the debt would be repaid—and once paid, the bill would be literally crossed out and cancelled. Even the word 'cancelled' carried a powerful picture with it. It referred to the practice of washing out the writing on a papyrus scroll so that it could be used again. But notice how all this will be accomplished, according to Paul: 'nailing it to the cross' (v 14). We cannot escape the conclusion, and Paul does not intend us to: Whatever is accomplished for our salvation, it will be through the cross.

How is atonement made?

When the mercy of God meets his wrath, it is not by a fickle dismissing of the severity of sin or an arbitrary decision to overlook evil. On the contrary, the holiness of God must be satisfied in a just way. That way was to be through the cross, but the sacrifices of the Old Testament were intended as a preparation, so that through ceremonies and symbols God explained beforehand the meaning of the cross.

THE DAY OF ATONEMENT IN THE OLD TESTAMENT

There are three words that are indivisible in the language of salvation: repentance, forgiveness and reconciliation. These three can never be separated, they must always be in this order and no two can properly exist without the third. But the gravity of the breach between the human race and God is such that, in order to draw attention to this seriousness, God demanded a blood sacrifice to make possible the reconciliation that he so desired. Thus, when a man brought his sacrifice to the priest for it to be slaughtered on his behalf, it demonstrated his recognition of sin and his sorrow for it.

The fact that the man who came with his sacrifice placed his hands on the head of the animal as the priest slaughtered it (Leviticus 1:4), was a picture of two things in particular: an acknowledgement of guilt and a recognition of the transfer of sin and its punishment. That the animal was understood to be a substitute is beyond any reasonable doubt, especially in the light of Leviticus 17:11, 'The life of a creature is in the blood, and I have given it to you to make atonement for yourselves on the altar; it is the blood that makes atonement for one's life.' Some see this as nothing more than an act of personal dedication to God, but we must ask that if this is so, why the need for an animal to be slaughtered, and how do we account for the clear meaning of the two goats of the Day of Atonement?

To discover how atonement for sin was provided under the old covenant, we will use the example of the great Day of Atonement described in Leviticus 16. All the Israelite sacrifices came to a climax on that day. The high priest brought two goats as a sacrifice on behalf of the nation. Every sacrifice was intended to speak of a man's repentance, but the goat slaughtered on the Day of Atonement represented national repentance, and when the second goat was released into the desert, it was a picture that the sins forgiven would never be returned against the people. The second animal was sent off into the wilderness as a 'scapegoat'; this was Tyndale's translation of a Hebrew word the meaning of which is still uncertain. This goat 'will carry on itself all their sins to a solitary place' (v 22).

The Septuagint (the Greek translation of the Old Testament completed around 250 BC) employs the word *hilasterion* (or related forms) no fewer than eighteen times in this chapter where it is translated 'atonement' in our English versions. The death of that animal turned away the just anger of God against the sins of the nation.

The instructions are precise, and the true meaning is given. The high priest would: 'Confess over it all the wickedness and rebellion of the

Israelites—all their sins—and put them on the goat's head. He shall send the goat away into the desert ... The goat will carry on itself all their sins to a solitary place' (Leviticus 16:21–22). Both the sacrificed goat and the released goat were pictures of the transference of sin—a substitute death and the removal of all guilt. Both were substitutes for the corporate life of the nation under the judgement of God.

What is vital to understand is the fact that the goat that was slaughtered was killed in place of the people who deserved death for their sin; it was their atonement, a covering over of sin, and the blood was sprinkled on the lid of the Ark of the Covenant, the atonement cover. This was the *hilasterion* referred to in Hebrews 9:5; it was literally the 'place of propitiation'. But it was much more than just a covering over of sin: it was the means by which that sin could be covered. This necessitated the death of the goat. It is for this reason that the writer to the Hebrews declared: 'The law requires that nearly everything be cleansed with blood, and without the shedding of blood there is no forgiveness' (Hebrews 9:22). The 'nearly everything' here refers to the fact that implements used in the services were purified by fire or water (Numbers 31:22–23), and clothes were to be washed (Leviticus 16:28)—but no exceptions were made for the offerings for sin.

Complementary to this, the animal that was released into the desert guaranteed the forgiveness of the nation's sin by God. That was God's response to their repentance. Reconciliation was the result of forgiveness, which in itself was possible because the just anger of God against sin had been satisfied. In theological language it was a 'penal substitution'.

The warning of death as a consequence of disobedience to God was a familiar theme for the Israelites: they knew the warning to Adam, and this was continued into the laws of the nation (Ezekiel 18:4,20). The only way that anyone could avoid the Judgement of God was by the offering of the life of a lamb, goat or bull in place of their own life. Every sacrifice that involved the death of an animal was intended to show the people how serious sin is, and what a devastating effect it has. But in addition, it would warn that, in order to be a just and holy God, he must and will punish sin with the sentence of death. The only way to avoid this was by the sacrifice of an animal as a substitute.

The Israelites also knew that propitiation, satisfying the righteous wrath of God, sprang from the love of God. Just as forgiveness only has meaning when a wrong has been committed and the one wronged is somehow satisfied, so propitiation only has meaning when the guilty stand under a just sentence and that sentence is carried out or averted. The Israelites were aware that the entire sacrificial system was a covenant of love by Yahweh who had entered into a relationship with them as with no other nation. There was no other explanation than love, for God's choice of Israel as his own special possession: 'The Lord appeared to us in the past, saying: "I have loved you with an everlasting love; I have drawn you with loving-kindness"' (Jeremiah 31:3, also Malachi 1:2). This reflected back to the beginning of his covenant where God encouraged the nation never to forget that,

The Lord did not set his affection on you and choose you because you were more numerous than other peoples, for you were the fewest of all peoples. But it was because the Lord loved you (Deuteronomy 7:7).

However, and this is the crucial point in the whole discussion of atonement, though the death of the animal was a picture of punishment, it was not really punishment—it was simply a picture, a symbol of punishment. Hebrews 10:1 describes all that happened under the ceremonial law—and this includes the slaughter of the sacrificial animal—as a 'shadow of the good things that are coming'. We all know that a shadow is not the reality. When we are exposed to the searing rays of the sun, what we long for is shelter to protect us; we look for a shadow and express our relief at 'standing in the shade'. We know well enough that the shade is not the real thing that is protecting us, it is merely a reflection of the reality—the tree or building that provides the escape from the burning sun. This is precisely the meaning of the Old Testament ceremonies.

The writer to the Hebrews rightly claimed that it is impossible for the blood of bulls and goats to take away sin (Hebrews 10:4). But were they then a complete waste of time? Not at all: the animal sacrifices not only reminded the people of the seriousness of sin and its consequences (Hebrews 10:3), but they were also God's appointed means of demonstrating that his anger against sin was satisfied, appeased, and that the one who offered the sacrifice and those he represented, whether family or nation, were forgiven and reconciled to God. But the sacrifices were only signposts to a final destination.

How could animals possibly atone for the sins of men and women? Imagine a man condemned for a terrible crime and the judge sentences him to life imprisonment with a recommendation of a minimum of thirty years. In response the condemned prisoner pleads: 'Well Sir, here is my dog, please put him away instead of me; it will be cheaper in every way, and besides, dogs generally do not live for thirty years.' Is that acceptable? Of course not. A dog cannot take the punishment of a man. The law would become a fool if ever that was an acceptable alternative. No more could an animal in the Old Testament take the punishment of a man. Even though for centuries, God ordered his people to offer animal sacrifices as a picture of the punishment they deserved, the apostle Paul tells us that, 'God left the sins committed beforehand unpunished' (Romans 3:25). They were forgiven, but without the just punishment that sin deserved.

How can this be the case? The following verse provides the answer: 'He did it to demonstrate his justice at the present time.' Those are terrible words: 'to demonstrate his justice'! We should tremble at that. What if God had demonstrated his justice all through the Old Testament by punishing sin as it deserved? When David committed that double sin of adultery and then murder he knew that there was no forgiveness under the old covenant—the punishment was death. And when Abraham lied and Moses lost his temper, what hope was there for any of them if God punished sins as they deserved to be punished? The only hope was the death of the sacrificial animal as a substitute. And yet, as the Scriptures make clear, no animal can properly die as a substitute for the sins of a man; it can only be a picture, a symbol—a shadow.

Atonement in the New Testament

We can turn to the New Testament to discover precisely what it claims for the life and death of Jesus Christ. If it is of 'first importance' that Christ died for our sins (1 Corinthians 15:3), why did it have to be the Son of God who died, and in what way was he a substitute for us?

WHY 'THE DIVINE SUBSTITUTE'?

Put plainly the answer is: to reverse all the consequences of the Fall. Ultimately the cause of the misery and suffering experienced in life, is the result of Satan's control over the lives of all who are born into this world (2 Corinthians 4:4; Colossians 1:13; 1 John 5:18–19). This does not excuse the human race for its rebellion, but it is the most comprehensive explanation of it. God became man in the person of his Son Jesus so that he might 'destroy the devil's work' (1 John 3:8). Throughout his life, death and resurrection Christ was, as Sinclair Ferguson has so rightly observed, 'multi-tasking'.[12] He came to reverse *everything* that Satan accomplished.

The atonement did not simply begin and end on a cross outside a city wall. Every aspect of the life of the incarnate Christ was intended as a reversal of the work of the devil. This is precisely why there was unusual satanic activity across Palestine during the three years of Christ's ministry; we must not assume that there was, or normally are, so many people possessed by evil spirits in such a small patch of land. It was Satan's last chance, and he threw everything at the Son of God.

It is often claimed that 'Christ came to die', but that is only part of the truth, he came to live also. His life, as well as his death and resurrection, are all related to the atonement.

Four key reasons for the sending of the Divine Substitute stand out:

The Divine Substitute shows us what God is like

Through the Fall of the human race, minds were held in darkness to the truth: a clear view of God was needed. The Fall masked the evidence of the eternal power and divine nature of God seen in Creation (Romans 1:20). It also clouded the sense of eternity that God placed in the heart of mankind (Ecclesiastes 3:11), and distorted the conscience that all possess (Romans 2:15). In all these, there is sufficient evidence for people to turn to God, but sin has tragically marred them all. Even God's perfect and pure laws, revealed through Israel as a reflection of his own character, were either dismissed as belonging only to the Jews, or disobeyed.

---

12 An expression used in **S. Ferguson's** Keswick Lecture, 'The Heart of the Gospel', Keswick Convention, July 2005, also delivered at the Evangelical Ministry Assembly in London 2005.

In the incarnation, God came to show what he is really like. To a human race that had degenerated into reproducing gods in its own likeness or that of 'birds and animals and reptiles' (Romans 1:23), the Son of God revealed the heart of God.

Jesus made the startling but simple statement: 'Anyone who has seen me has seen the Father' (John 14:9). This was either the most arrogantly blasphemous assertion ever made by a man, or else it was true. There is no middle way here. Jesus claimed that to hear his words, to watch his actions, to learn from his compassion, to receive his forgiveness and to observe his life, is to hear, watch, learn, receive and observe the very character of God himself.

One New Testament writer asserted, 'The Son is the radiance of God's glory and the exact representation of his being' (Hebrews 1:3)—meaning that the Son is the exact character of the actual reality of God himself. Jesus was not the reflection of his Father, as the rays of the sun glancing off a mirror or the glory reflected in the face of Moses, he was the perfect character of God. All that Jesus was, God is. There is no greater exhibition of the love, compassion, mercy, and holiness of God than Jesus Christ. When we admire his glory, we admire the glory of the Father also.

This perfect and ultimate revelation of God is highly relevant to the atonement as a demonstration of the love of God.

The Divine Substitute shows us what we are like

As the filthiness of a soiled garment is shown up against the pure whiteness of snow, so the perfect life of Christ reveals to all the human race how far short of the glory of God it falls (Romans 3:23). This too is a revelation of God's grace in the incarnation and equally a demonstration of the atoning love of God. When Peter knelt in the boat and cried out: 'Go away from me, Lord; I am a sinful man!' (Luke 5:8), it was a natural response to the holiness of Jesus. The Gospels record other examples of those who drew back from the holy character of Christ, and perhaps no more so than when the arresting party fell down at the presence of Christ in the Garden of Gethsemane (John 18:6).

Those who suggest that the gospel should not present men and women as sinful beyond human repair, forget that when anyone comes face to face with Jesus Christ, that is exactly how they feel. In fact, without this, there is no hope of salvation. The wonderful compassion and care of Jesus convicts us of our own failure to follow his example, and more deeply, our own personal rebellion and impurity.

If one task of the Holy Spirit is to convict the world of sin and righteousness and judgement (John 16:8), he will do this pre-eminently by directing our attention to Christ.

The Divine Substitute shows us what we should be like

Through the incarnation, God by his grace reveals his own character, and how far short the human race falls from this. Christ's life is a visible demonstration of the holiness that pleases God. He came as the 'last Adam' (1 Corinthians 15:22) to fulfil all that the first Adam so lamentably failed to do. Christ fulfilled the law perfectly (Matthew 5:17). The word 'fulfil' in this verse has been the subject of much debate. Of course, he fulfilled the law by explaining its fuller meaning and by demonstrating that it pointed to himself. But it must also mean that he kept the law fully. He was 'without sin' (Hebrews 4:15) and pleased his Father perfectly (Matthew 3:17). All this, the first Adam failed to do and the last Adam accomplished.

When Peter encouraged the scattered Christians to stand firm in the approaching persecution, he offered Christ as their great model to follow:

To this you were called, because Christ suffered for you, leaving you an example, that you should follow in his steps. 'He committed no sin, and no deceit was found in his mouth.' When they hurled their insults at him, he did not retaliate; when he suffered, he made no threats. Instead, he entrusted himself to him who judges justly (1 Peter 2:21–23).

So too, on the subject of forgiveness, once again he is our pattern: 'Be kind and compassionate to one another, forgiving each other, just as in Christ God forgave you' (Ephesians 4:32). Even in marital relationships, Paul turned to Christ as a perfect example of love: 'Husbands, love your wives, just as Christ loved the church and gave himself up for her' (Ephesians 5:25).

The Master himself encouraged his disciples to 'learn from me, for I am gentle and humble in heart' (Matthew 11:28). It is proper for a Christian to ask in any and every situation: 'What would Jesus do now?' All his teaching was his way of explaining in a practical, down-to-earth manner, exactly what the Father expects of us. This was all related to the atonement, for he came to destroy the works of the devil.

However, although it is true that Christ is our example, it is equally true that it is an impossible example! His compassion and love, his purity and self-control, his selfless devotion to others, and his total commitment to the cause of his Father exemplified, beyond the possibility of our imitation, what it means to 'Love the Lord your God with all your heart and with all your soul and with all your mind ... and ... your neighbour as yourself' (Matthew 22:37–38).

Those whose theology of the atonement stops short of the cross, and who believe that the life and ministry of Christ are seen solely in his character as a model for us to follow—a moral example—are confronted with an impossible dilemma: if it is true that the rescue plan of God was to send his Son simply to show us how to live, then we are all doomed to tragic failure. Besides, why did he die in the manner that he did?

Above all, the Divine Substitute died on a cross

This is why the cross was needed. This is 'of first importance' to the gospel message. Yet this emphasis on the cross earned ridicule for the Christians among the Romans. A piece of first century graffiti pictures a donkey-headed man spread-eagled on a cross. It was considered a joke, hilarious, that anyone should form a religion around a criminal who was put to death in the most degrading and vicious manner that the Romans could devise. Unless the apostles knew that something took place on the cross that was essential to salvation, and without which there could be no reconciliation with God—no destroying of the works of Satan—then they would surely have played down the manner of his death.

Why did Paul declare that he would never boast 'except in the *cross* of our Lord Jesus' (Galatians 6:14)?

Why did he determine to know nothing 'except Jesus Christ and him *crucified*' (1 Corinthians 2:2)?

Why was he so fearful that 'the *cross* of Christ be emptied of its power' (1 Corinthians 1:17)?

For what other reason than this did he stand by a message of the *cross* that he admitted was both 'a stumbling block' and 'foolishness' (1 Corinthians 1:23)?

Why did he admit openly to the 'offence of the *cross*' (Galatians 5:11)?

There were even those in New Testament times who were already changing the gospel to avoid being 'persecuted for the *cross* of Christ' (Galatians 6:12).

The apostle was well aware of the danger of this insistence on the cross when he admitted that Jesus was obedient to death 'even death on a *cross*' (Philippians 2:8). Paul could have stopped at 'death', but he deliberately emphasised the manner of that death. Similarly, elsewhere Christ 'endured the *cross*, scorning its shame' (Hebrews 12:2).

What was accomplished on the cross, and how it was accomplished, was of overwhelming significance to the apostles. They saw that it was vital to the Christian faith.

With increasing urgency during his ministry, Jesus himself foretold his death and the circumstances surrounding it, not least the resurrection that would follow (Matthew 12:40;16:21; 17:9,22–23; 20:18–19; 21:38–40). The Gospel writers dedicate a large proportion of their records to the last week in the life of Jesus including his resurrection. In the case of John, this amounts to well over a third of his Gospel.

Why the Divine Substitute died on the cross

There are many words that are used in the New Testament to describe what Christ accomplished on the cross, such as ransom, sacrifice, reconciliation, cleansing, destroying the works of the devil. But at the heart of the atonement is a word found in Romans 3:25 and elsewhere. It was the word that proved so vital to the conversion of James Gardiner in our introductory story:

Whom God hath set forth *to be* a propitiation through faith in his blood, to declare his righteousness for the remission of sins that are past, through the forbearance of God.

Propitiation is a hugely significant word, and some modern translations have had difficulty in representing it in modern English.

The Authorised Version of the Bible accurately translates the original word as 'propitiation', but the term is little used now, and needs explanation. However, the Revised Version, the New American Standard Bible, the New King James Version and the English Standard Version all retain the word 'propitiation'.

The Revised Standard Version replaces it with the word 'expiation', which hardly clarifies it for the modern reader, and certainly betrays a very different understanding of the concept that Paul had in mind.

The Good News Bible substitutes a long sentence: 'God offered him so that by his death he should become the means by which people's sins are forgiven' which is so vague that it is not even a helpful paraphrase.

The New International Version places the phrase 'a sacrifice of atonement' in the text and adds an explanatory note: 'as the one who would turn aside his wrath, taking away sin'; their footnote is accurate, but their text is misleading.

The Living Bible excels itself with a remarkably good paraphrase: 'To take the punishment for our sins and to end all God's anger against us.' Admittedly that is a mouthful to translate just one word, but it certainly brings out the meaning of the word that Paul originally used.

The New English Bible renders a similar form of this word in 1 John 2:2 as a vague 'remedy for the defilement of our sins.'

The struggles of the translators to handle the word, at least illustrate that it is undoubtedly an unfamiliar word to most readers today. However, because it is such a significant word, it is wiser to leave it in the text and allow a footnote to explain it, if only because there is no English word that can double for it.

Words from the root 'to propitiate' appear on only a few occasions in the New Testament. The following references are taken from the English Standard Version.

In Romans 3:25, the word that Paul used in the Greek is the word *hilasterion*. It is a noun and refers to *the place of propitiation*. It appears only here and in Hebrews 9:5 'Above the Ark were the Cherubim of the Glory, overshadowing the atonement cover'. Here we have the noun ('atonement cover') which many versions unhelpfully translate by 'the mercy seat' whereas more literally it would be: 'the propitiation'. The use of 'mercy seat' reflects the translation of an Old Testament word that we will come to later.

Another form of the same noun is used in 1 John 2:2 'He is the propitiation for our sins, and not for ours only but also for the sins of the whole world', and 1 John 4:10 'This is love, not that we have loved God but that he loved us and sent his Son to be the propitiation for our sins.' The word John used is *hilasmos*, and it is more properly understood as *the means of propitiation*.

On just two occasions the verb is used. In Hebrews 2:17 'He had to be made like his brothers in every respect, so that he might become a merciful and faithful high priest in the service of God, to make propitiation for the sins of the people', the root verb is *hilaskomai*, and the infinitive here means simply *to make propitiation*. Finally, there is an interesting use of the verb in the parable of the rich man and the tax collector (Luke 18:13). Whilst most translations render the tax collector's response as something like 'God, have mercy on me', the word 'mercy' is not used here. Mercy is *eleos* in Greek (as for example in Matthew 9:13), whilst the word used here is the passive imperative form of the verb *hilaskomai*. The tax man prayed, 'God be propitious to me'. That, as we will see, is something other than mercy.

All the standard lexicons agree that the word *hilasterion* refers to that which appeases, placates, expiates, propitiates.[13] However, because we are not familiar with the word propitiation today, to gain an understanding of the meaning of the word there are two directions we can look to for help.

PROPITIATION IN THE MIND OF THE FIRST CENTURY PAGAN

In writing to the Christians at Rome, Paul was well aware that many of his readers were converts from paganism, and that they would have an immediate handle on the word propitiation. For the Greeks and Romans their gods influenced every part of life from birth to the grave. With this in

---

13 See for example **Grimm/Thayer,** *Greek Lexicon* (Edinburgh: T&T Clark, 1892) and that of **Walter Bauer,** *Greek Lexicon,* trans. Arndt & Gingrich (Bauer) (Chicago: University of Chicago Press, 1979).

mind, each person had to keep their favourite gods and goddesses 'on side'. But religion was not a personal relationship with the gods, and a bond of love was virtually unknown. It is true that the Greeks spoke of Zeus (known to the Romans as Jupiter) as 'kindly Zeus' and even 'father', and there are references and inscriptions to 'dear' gods, but this was more a matter of respect than affection. As one classical scholar has expressed it: 'No Greek would ever have thought of keeping a spiritual diary'[14]. Nor, we may add, was there anything in the writing of pagan devotees of the gods comparable to the deep expressions of love and loyalty that we find in the psalms of David, and certainly nothing that approaches the warm love and commitment to Christ reflected in the New Testament in such expressions as: 'Though you have not seen him, you love him; and even though you do not see him now, you believe in him and are filled with an inexpressible and glorious joy' (1 Peter 1:8) and Paul's longing 'That I may know him ...' (Philippians 3:10 AV).

In the first century, keeping on the right side of the gods was achieved not so much by personal devotion as in community worship; religion was firmly in the hands of the local municipality. It was the duty of the authorities to put on a good show for the entertainment of the gods; this was done through impressive musical and theatrical festivals, elaborate religious ceremonies (the Elgin Marbles that once adorned the Parthenon in Athens depict the celebration of Athena's birthday), and athletic competitions (such was the origin of the Olympic games); even the butchery of the gladiatorial contests was offered to the gods.

For their part, the gods offered no moral standards, no absolute laws, and no example of integrity. On the contrary, their own behaviour was often scandalous:

- There might you see the gods in sundry shapes
- Committing heady riots, incest, rapes.[15]

Although the gods did punish some offences—particularly against parents,

---

14 R. Parker, *Oxford History of the Classical World* (Oxford: Oxford University Press, 1988), Art. 'Greek Religion', p. 261.

15 Parker, *Oxford History of the Classical World,* p. 261.

guests, the dead and breaking oaths—virtually the only religious crime was offending the community by not worshipping the gods it had chosen to worship. This was the crime of Socrates since he did not 'recognise the gods that the city recognised', and later it was a significant reason for the persecution of Christians; they were dubbed 'atheists' (*atheoi*) for refusing the traditional gods. The concept of atonement, that was clear in the Jewish and Christian faiths, was unknown to the pagan, since sin was only failure and there was virtually no conception of infringement of a moral law that had been established by the gods.

Whilst there was no sense of personal love and commitment to the gods, such as Christianity taught in the relationship to Christ, worship was still a pact between the individual and the gods, and for the worshipper to break his part of the agreement would bring severe punishment upon crops, family, or health. Religious ritual in the various ceremonies was detailed and exacting, and to fail in one aspect would bring displeasure from the gods with severe consequences.

Both the Romans and the Greeks viewed their gods generally as not kindly disposed towards the human race, and the worshipper's task was to bring them into a favourable frame of mind. Someone has compared it to a boy chatting up a girl. The worshipper had to 'chat-up' these gods and impress them; to soothe their feelings in order to get them in the right attitude, so that instead of feeling badly disposed, they would be friendly. The principle was referred to as one of *do ut des*, 'I give so that you will give'. This was not thought of as bribery so much as each keeping their side of the bargain. It was generally agreed that 'Gifts persuade the gods, gifts revere (honour) kings'. The gods needed persuading. In popular religion, it was strictly a reciprocal relationship between men and the gods. Admittedly Plato condemned this as reducing worship to an act of merchandise between gods and men; he saw it as equivalent to seducing the gods 'by presents like a villainous money lender'[16]—but Plato held a minority view.

---

[16] See **Walter Woodburn Hyde,** *Greek Religion and its Survivals* (New York: Cooper Square Publishers. 1963), pp. 35–36.

One thing was certain, the gods—most of whom lived as 'a sprawling family' in the palace of Zeus on Mount Olympus—ruled the universe for their own benefit and not for ours. There was no religious organization among the Greeks or Romans that could develop a moral code or even impose theological orthodoxy—not that either the gods or their consorts were greatly interested in either morality or orthodoxy. Nor would they do anything for mere mortals unless and until they were appeased: 'It was unusual to pray seriously without making an offering of some kind ... or promising to make one should the prayer be fulfilled.'[17] Mankind must take the initiative and make the offerings in order to propitiate the gods and earn their good will. Here 'propitiate' refers to turning away their bad feelings. George Smeaton, Professor of Exegetics at the Free Church College in Edinburgh towards the end of the nineteenth century and a renowned scholar, was unequivocal: 'The uniform acceptance of the word [propitiation] in classical Greek, when applied to the Deity, is the means of appeasing God, or of averting His anger; and not a single instance to the contrary occurs in the whole of Greek literature.'[18]

In the ancient world, even when the word *hilasterion* was used of human relationships without any reference to the deities, it always referred to a payment as compensation by which the hurt party is appeased and the two are reconciled. It is clear that in the first century, and for a long time before, *hilasterion* and its related words always had to do with the anger of the one offended being soothed or satisfied by the offender. It is important to add to this that, 'The Bible writers have nothing to do with pagan conceptions of a capricious and vindictive deity inflicting arbitrary punishments on offending worshippers, who must then bribe him back to a good mood by the appropriate offerings.'[19]

We might also notice that the Old Testament frequently mocked the gods of the nations (see e.g. Psalm 135:15–18; Isaiah 40:18–20) whose anger was irrational, since they could not see, hear or think, and they set no moral

---

17 Hyde, *Greek Religion and its Survivals,* pp. 264, 271.

18 G. Smeaton, *The Apostles' Doctrine of the Atonement* (Edinburgh: 1870), p. 455.

19 L. Morris, *The Apostolic Preaching of the Cross* (London: Tyndale Press, 1955), p. 129.

standards that could be broken; at the best their anger was selfish and capricious. This is somewhat humorously illustrated in the ancient Atrahasis Epic from perhaps shortly after the time of Abraham. This is a Babylonian story of a great flood. Anu ruled in heaven, whilst Enlil controlled the minor gods on earth; the human race was created when these minor deities went on strike and refused to work. Unfortunately, the noise from the rapidly increasing human race gave Enlil a headache and so he brought a great flood on the earth to settle accounts.[20] According to the Bible, the cause of the Flood in the time of Noah was based upon very different criteria.

With all this in mind, we can now run through those uses of the word propitiation in the New Testament and watch for a significant difference from the pagan understanding:

Romans 3:25 'Christ Jesus, whom God put forward as a propitiation by his blood.'

Hebrews 2:17 'He had to ... make propitiation for the sins of the people.'

1 John 2:2. 'He is the propitiation for our sins ...'

1 John 4:10. 'God ... sent his Son to be the propitiation for our sins.'

And the cry of the tax man in Luke 18:13, which we may translate as 'God, be propitious to me, the sinner.'

The difference is clear. Whatever propitiation means, the initiative, the plan, and carrying out of the plan, all belong to God. It is God who provides the propitiation. That was unknown in pagan religion. For the converted pagans, Paul did here with the word propitiation what he frequently took delight in doing elsewhere: he took a common word and clothed it with a brand new Christian distinction.[21]

We have not yet arrived at the true meaning of the word, but we know that in the Christian faith, it is not us doing something for God, but God doing it for us through his Son. We do not propitiate God, because we

---

20 H.W.F. Saggs, *The Babylonians* (London: The Folio Society, 1999), pp. 325–328.

21 A contrary view of the meaning of propitiation to the one taken in this book will be found in Diesler, *Paul's Letter to the Romans.* London: SCM Press, 1989), pp. 115–116. For a summary of some of the contemporary arguments about the word *hilasterion* see **Douglas Moo** on Romans in *The Wycliffe Exegetical Commentary* (Chicago: Moody Press, 1991), pp.232–238.

cannot; rather, God provides propitiation. That shift in understanding became a hallmark of true Christianity.

PROPITIATION IN THE MIND OF THE FIRST CENTURY JEW

Some of the Christians at Rome were converted Jews, and they would have had an altogether different understanding of the word propitiation from their pagan neighbours; and theirs was more precisely the meaning that Paul had in mind. Although to link Paul's use of the word with the Old Testament concept of atonement has long been dismissed as 'fanciful and inadequate',[22] nevertheless that is precisely what we must do. Paul would have expected his Jewish readers to think along the lines of the Hebrew Scriptures. Remember that 'Christ died for our sins *according to the Scriptures*' (1 Corinthians 15:3). We therefore cannot appreciate the significance of the cross without an understanding of atonement under the older covenant.[23]

Among the furniture in the Tabernacle was the 'Ark of the Covenant'. This was a box made from acacia wood and overlaid with gold both inside and out, and with a lid of pure gold on which two gold cherubim were mounted (Exodus 25:10–22). In the Hebrew, this lid for the Ark is called *kapporeth*, which comes from the word *kipper* (atonement) and occurs twenty-seven times in the Old Testament. The Authorised Version, among others, translates it as 'the mercy seat', although neither the words 'mercy' nor 'seat' are in the original.[24] The Greek translation of the Old Testament (the Septuagint), used the word *hilasterion* in Exodus 25:17 to identify this lid. 'Atonement cover' (as the NIV) is a fairly adequate translation, though

---

22 J. Hastings, *Dictionary of the Apostolic Church* (Edinburgh: T & T Clark. 1918), **Frederic Platt** art. on 'Propitiation'.

23 The symposium ed. by **David Peterson,** *Where Wrath and Mercy Meet* (Carlisle: Paternoster, 2001), provides a more detailed study of this whole subject and from the same perspective.

24 *Theological Word Book of the Old Testament* (Chicago: Moody Press, 1980), Vol. 1, p. 453 states simply 'The word, however, was not related to mercy, and of course was not a seat. The word is derived from the root "to atone"'.

'propitiation cover' would be even closer to the meaning. In Hebrews 9:5 it is referred to as the '*hilasterion*' (NIV 'atonement cover'), which unfortunately is obscured by most translations when they insist on the phrase 'mercy seat' (as the AV, NKJV and ESV). Whilst 'mercy seat' is a beautiful expression, and has found its way into the literature, hymns and prayer life of Christians for centuries, it obscures the real meaning of the original word and it is therefore disappointing that it has persisted so long as a translation. William Tyndale led the way by using the phrase 'a seat of mercy' in his 1526 English New Testament to translate the word *hilasterion* in Romans 3:25.

This Ark of the Covenant was kept in the inner sanctuary of the Tabernacle, and at the great annual ceremony on the Day of Atonement—and on this day alone—the blood of sacrifice was sprinkled by the high priest seven times on the propitiatory cover. This day, which is still celebrated among Jews as *yom kippur*, is first referred to in Leviticus 23:27 where in the Greek translation of the Old Testament, the word for 'propitiation' is used. Any Christian Jew listening to the reading of Paul's letter would, without a doubt, have in mind that propitiatory cover when he heard the word *hilasterion*. It was the key place where the blood of the sacrifice was sprinkled on the Day of Atonement, just once a year. This was the most solemn of all the Jewish ceremonies. The sacrificial offering was a death in the place of the one who offered it. It was a substitute—a vicarious sacrifice—not simply a life offered as a representative, but a life taken as a substitute.

We have established just two very important facts about the word *hilasterion*. First, for the converted pagan in the congregation at Rome it referred to the efforts he and his community made to bring the gods on side. Second, for the converted Jew it brought to mind the place of propitiation in the Tabernacle. However, the difference between these two approaches was fundamental. The pagan was never given a good reason why the gods required these offerings, or why they were not in a happier frame of mind. By contrast, the Jew had a high view of God as awesomely pure and who was to be feared by all who stepped outside the detail of his law. The pagan had to appease the gods simply because they were more powerful, whereas the Jew made his offerings because God was not only powerful, but graciously loving as well as immensely holy.

Psalm 66 is a magnificent example of how joy, praise, the awesome power of God, the offering of sacrifices and the gracious love of an ever-listening creator are all mingled together in one outpouring of the psalmist's experience (see especially vs 1–3, 13–15, 19–20). Nothing equivalent to this appears in pagan literature.

With this background we can turn our attention specifically to the cross of Christ.

THE SACRIFICE OF CHRIST

There can be no doubt that Christ associated his coming explicitly with the sacrificial system. He identified himself with the servant in Isaiah 53 (Luke 22:37) where the sacrificial language of the prophet is unmistakable, and he claimed to have come to 'give his life a ransom for many' (Mark 10:45)—an expression that to the mind of his Jewish disciples would have undoubtedly awakened thoughts of the history of their religion (Exodus 13:13–15). In the Passover meal with the Twelve, Christ was clearly presenting himself as the final Passover lamb. Whilst it is denied by those who object to any link with sacrifice in the Last Supper, it is certainly unlikely that such phrases as: 'This cup is the new covenant in my blood, which is poured out for many for the forgiveness of sins' (Luke 22:20 and Matthew 26:28) would have no connection in the minds of the disciples with the sacrifices of the first Passover.

Similarly Jesus must have been looking forward to this meal with his disciples when much earlier he declared:

I tell you the truth, unless you can eat the flesh of the Son of Man and drink his blood, you have no life in you. Whoever eats my flesh and drinks my blood has eternal life, and I will raise him up at the last day. For my flesh is real food and my blood is real drink. Whoever eats my flesh and drinks my blood remains in me, and I in him (John 6:53–56).

Whatever else that passage means, it is the language of sacrifice, and at least in retrospect the disciples would have understood it that way. John the Baptist knew this in his claim 'Look, the Lamb of God, who takes away the sin of the world!' (John 1:29). However we translate Revelation 13:8, John the apostle was certain that Christ was the 'Lamb slain'.

Clearly Christ had much more to teach his disciples about his death, but it would be 'more than you can now bear' (John 16:12). Not until his death and resurrection had shattered their insistence that his triumph would be with a crown and not a cross, could they fully understand the absolute necessity of Golgotha. Not until he had risen from the dead could Jesus show his disciples 'in all the Scriptures' (Luke 24:25–27) the true significance of the recent events. Similarly, it is not possible to read the letter to the Hebrews without appreciating that Christ fulfilled all the ceremonies and sacrifices of the Old Testament. To read the life and death of Christ and to divorce our understanding of it from the Old Testament religious system is a tragic spiritual and hermeneutical blindness.

As we have earlier stated, the most significant phrase to explain the death of Christ is found at the end of Romans 3:25: 'He [God] had left the sins committed beforehand unpunished.' All through the Old Testament, thousands of sacrifices were offered and tens of thousands of animals were slaughtered in ceremonial ritual. On each occasion it was a picture of how seriously God views sin and, mercifully, how willing he is to forgive. God was illustrating for the people that he cannot wink at sin and simply turn his back on it. Thus, throughout the Old Testament period, sin was forgiven for those who repented, but no one had taken the punishment those sins deserved.

In his classic book on the subject of the atonement, James Denney wrote: 'If the propitiatory death of Jesus is eliminated from the love of God, it might be unfair to say that the love of God is robbed of all meaning, but it is certainly robbed of its apostolic meaning.'[25] When Paul and John wrote of the death of Christ in terms of 'a propitiation for our sins', they could have only one chief end in focus, and that was that Christ died to fulfil all those shadows offered throughout the Old Testament period. And remember, they were offered to appease or placate the just anger of God against sin. John the Baptist surely understood this when he announced Jesus of Nazareth as 'The *Lamb* of God, who takes away the sin of the world' (John 1:29).

A vicarious sacrifice
However scandalous the theme of Christ taking our blame and punishment

---

25 J. Denney, *The Death of Christ* (1903) (London: Tyndale Press, 1951), p. 152.

may be, it is clearly the longed-for promise under the old covenant and the fulfilled conviction of the new. What else could Paul logically have meant when he claimed the sins committed beforehand were left unpunished 'to demonstrate his justice at the present time' (Romans 3:26)? The death of Christ was the ultimate demonstration of the justice of God—and God's justice and love are inseparable.

The Scriptures are in no doubt that in some sense the sins of many are placed on Christ. In what is arguably the clearest passage about vicarious sacrifice in the whole of the Old Testament, Isaiah 53 refers to the fact that 'The Lord has laid on him the iniquity of us all' (v 6), so that the Messiah becomes 'a guilt offering' (v 10); in this way he 'bore the sin of many' (v 12). It was in this sense also that John the Baptist understood Christ as 'The Lamb of God, who takes away the sin of the world' (John 1:29), and that Paul saw God making him 'to be sin for us' (2 Corinthians 5:21) and Christ 'was sacrificed once to take away the sins of many people' (Hebrews 9:28). Peter similarly understood that 'He himself bore our sins in his body on the tree' (1 Peter 2:24).

The writer to the Hebrews tells us that he 'provided purification for sins' (1:3), 'obtained eternal redemption' (9:12), came to 'do away with sin by the sacrifice of himself' (9:26), and was 'sacrificed once to take away the sins of many' (9:28).

There is far too much in the letters of the New Testament that relate the death of Christ as a substitute for the sinner—this is known as a *vicarious* sacrifice—for this theme to be lightly denied.

A penal sacrifice

But the Scriptures go further. Isaiah ventured into the territory of God punishing the Messiah:

Stricken by God, smitten by him, and afflicted ... Pierced for our transgressions, crushed for our iniquities ... The punishment that brought us peace was upon him ... It was the Lord's will to crush him and cause him to suffer (Isaiah 53:4–5, 10).

Unless we deny that this chapter has anything to do with the Messiah as the Servant, it is hardly possible to understand it in any other way than referring to a vicarious punishment (the word penal refers to punishment), deliberately inflicted by the Father to cover the sins of many. Alec Motyer comments on the phrase: 'The Lord has laid on him the iniquity of us all' (Isaiah 53:6): 'The Servant suffers under our sin and under the Lord's hand ... his sufferings were the penalty which he paid for our transgressions ... In his Servant, the Lord was dealing with all that merited his wrath. The Servant is the lamb of God.'[26] Edward J Young took the same position: 'The iniquity of which we are guilty does not come back to meet and strike us as we might rightly expect, but rather strikes him in our stead ... The thought of violence is not entirely lacking ... he as our substitute bore the punishment that the guilt of our sins required.'[27]

When Paul wrote 'God made him who had no sin to be sin for us, so that in him we might become the righteousness of God' (2 Corinthians 5:21), he clearly had substitution in mind, and since Christ would become our sin, he must bear the penalty of that. Much has been written on the phrase 'to be sin'. The sentence literally reads: 'The (one) who knew no sin, for us was made sin'. This is not only a reference to the 'sin offering' of the Old Testament, but to the fact that even though he himself was wholly without sin, he was counted, and treated, as a sinner for our sake.

In Romans 8:1–3 Paul could hardly have laid the issue more plainly before his readers. Here he plays with two words from the same root. When Paul declared that there is 'no condemnation' for those who are in Christ Jesus, the noun *katakrima* refers to the sentence or penalty when it is carried out. Immediately Paul explained how this could be: God sent his own Son and 'condemned sin in the flesh' (Romans 8:3 ESV); this time the word is *katekrinen*, a verb that means not merely to examine a case but pronounce judgement. In other words, in his Son God pronounced and carried out the sentence that we deserve so that we are free from any penalty. He did this by making his Son a 'sin offering' (v 3). There can be no

---

26 A. Motyer, *The Prophecy of Isaiah* (Leicester: IVP, 1993), p. 429.

27 E.J. Young. *The Book of Isaiah* (Grand Rapids: Eerdmans, 1972), Vol. III p. 350.

doubt that we are expected to read this whole passage in the context of the Jewish sacrificial system.

Similarly, the word propitiation in Romans 3:25 is in the context of Paul having spent more than two chapters outlining the tragic diagnosis of the human race under the bondage of sin and the just wrath of God. The 'But now' of verse 21 is generally considered to be the turning point of the whole argument: Paul is now about to reveal the way by which the whole sad saga can be reversed. The solution lies in God's provision of his Son as a propitiation.

But what precisely is this? The responses to this question have ranged widely. Some would see it as no more than representing the human race to the Father. But if 'the wages of sin is death' (Romans 6:23) and Christ clearly had no reason to die, for he was without personal sin and guilt, then his death must surely be more than representative. Others believe that his death was intended as a 'moral impression' to show how God would punish sin and thus, hopefully, turn men away from transgressions. But this leaves open the vital question of what happens to the sins already committed? Are they atoned for by our own subsequent good works, and if so, we are back to the age old question of how many good works atone for bad ones?

C.H. Dodd, among others, viewed the word *hilasterion* as expiation and not propitiation: in other words it was only cancelling sin and not satisfying the wrath of God. He denied any idea of punishment in the cross, maintaining that the blood of sacrifice was never more than symbolic of a life presented as an offering to God, rather than some transaction taking place through the death.[28] On the contrary, Leon Morris has demonstrated that the word 'blood' would, above all, mean a violent death in the mind of

---

28 See **C.H. Dodd,** *The Bible and the Greeks* (London: Hodder and Stoughton, 1935), and *The Johannine Epistles* (London: Harper, 1945), on 1 John 2:2. His view was popular for some time and influenced the *New English Bible* translation. It is receiving renewed interest today. See more recently **Christopher Bryan,** *A Preface to the Romans: Notes on the Epistle in its Literary and Cultural Setting* Oxford: Oxford University Press, 2000), who sees propitiation as 'expiating or wiping away sin'.

the Hebrews. He showed that more than two-thirds of the use of the word in the Old Testament referred to a death by violence and not a life as an offering.[29]

Theologians on the same side of this debate differ as to whether 'to be sin' means that our *sinfulness* was transferred to Christ, which is certainly what Martin Luther implied,[30] or whether only the *guilt* and thus the punishment was transferred. The language of Luther is perhaps too extreme for many, even though it does full justice to the biblical phrase 'made sin'. A.A. Hodge attempted to clarify the phrase 'made him to be sin', so that Christ remains no less infinitely holy, harmless and undefiled: 'when the chastisement of our sins is upon him, or their legal responsibility counted his.'[31] Either way, we must insist that his death was a 'penal' substitution (i.e. to do with punishment) rather than a 'moral' substitution (i.e. to do with character).

Hodge emphasised that Christ did not actually become our sin, since he considered that 'the personal character of one man can never be transferred to another'; however, he did believe that our legal liability—a mass of broken laws and commandments—was transferred to Christ's account. Hodge was not wholly correct, for if the personal character (or qualities) of one cannot be transferred to another, then how can Christ's perfect righteousness be transferred to us? Yet Paul insists that in Christ we 'become the righteousness of God (2 Corinthians 5:21).

Thus, the death of Christ was a penal substitution, satisfying the full demand of the law against sin, but to do full justice to such a phrase as 'became sin' we must go further.

---

29 L. Morris, *The Apostolic Preaching of the Cross* (London: Tyndale Press, 1955), ch. 3. In this chapter he interacts with others in the same school as Dodd, such as Vincent Taylor, P.T. Forsyth, and especially Bishop Westcott.

30 Martin Luther on Galatians 3:13, *St Paul's Epistle to the Galatians* (1535) (London: James Clarke, 1961).

31 A.A. Hodge, *Outlines of Theology* ed. by W.H. Goold (London: T Nelson and Sons, 1872), p. 314.

A curse

The extent of Jesus bearing the just punishment for our sins must be what Paul had in mind when he introduced the terrible word 'curse' into the atonement: 'Christ redeemed us from the curse of the law by becoming a curse for us, for it is written: "Cursed is everyone who is hung on a tree"' (Galatians 3:13). Paul's quotation is from Deuteronomy 21:23, and it is both deliberate and potent: 'Anyone who is hung on a tree is under God's curse.'

Contained within the regulations given to Moses for the people, this was not a broad statement that hanging from a tree was intrinsically a thing cursed by God; it had a specific context which was a reference to those who are put to death when found guilty of a capital offence. Therefore, the thrust of what Paul was writing was not that Christ was somehow under the curse of God because the Romans crucified him 'on a tree', but that he had died under the judgement of a capital offence. The fact that in so doing he 'redeemed us' can hardly mean that the capital offence was that which the Roman authorities handed out to him. Paul had something far more terrible in mind. Whether we like the conclusion or not, it is virtually impossible to suggest that Paul meant anything other than the fact that Christ died under the righteous judgement of the Father against sin ('the curse of the law'), that we all justly deserve. Whilst it is always risky to build a theology on a preposition, the word 'for' in Galatians 3:13 (and in 2 Corinthians 5:21, 1 Timothy 2:6 etc) is *huper*, and is best understood as 'on behalf of' or 'for the sake of'—some prefer 'instead of'.

We must pause to consider that word 'curse'. The first and last uses of the word in the Old Testament (Genesis 3:14 and Malachi 2:2) clearly reveal that it is a Judgement of God upon sin. It was the result of Adam's fall into rebellion against his Creator. But in its various forms of verb and noun, it occurs more than 170 times and mostly with reference to God. Sixteen times the verb 'cursed' is used in Deuteronomy and all but four of those are in chapter 27. When the Levites who climbed Mount Ebal gave out the list of warnings that would accompany disobedience, they commenced each by the phrase 'cursed is the man'. Whilst the word is also used of men cursing men, whenever it is used of God, it refers to the result of sin and the punishment that follows. This must have been Paul's intention in Galatians 3:13—or else the apostle has deceived us by such a plain statement.

The words related to 'curse' in the New Testament carry the same meaning. Peter referred to those who have 'eyes full of adultery' and 'who never stop sinning', they are, he concluded 'an accursed brood!' (2 Peter 2:14); that is, those who will bear the appointed penalty that the curse of God implies. The archaeologist, Sir William Ramsay, discovered in a third century tomb in Phrygia, a significant threat to anyone who would break into the burial chamber: 'If anyone shall open the tomb, there shall be upon him the curses as many as are written in (the book), on his sight and his whole body and his children and his life.'[32] Clearly, the curse refers to a just Judgement on those who offend.

We may well ask, that if there was little more to Golgotha than death on a cross—that is, a physical experience of suffering—how does this account for such agony in Gethsemane that 'his sweat was like drops of blood falling to the ground' (Luke 22:44)? Thousands had been crucified before him, and many went courageously to their death; there must have been something full of dread that lay ahead for Christ. Only a proper understanding of the curse of God on Christ as the divine substitute for our guilt, sin and punishment could account for that terrible cry of abandonment: 'My God, my God, why have you forsaken me?' (Matthew 27:46). At that moment—the first and last in all eternity—there was a breach between the Father and the Son as Christ 'bore our sin in his body on the tree' and all the just punishment that went with it. At that precise time, and for the first time in the history of the human race, sin had been punished as it fully deserved, and for the first time the enormity of the sinfulness of sin was revealed—it required nothing less than the death of the Son of God to make a full and final atonement.

A propitiatory sacrifice
It is in the sense that Christ's death was a vicarious and penal sacrifice (a

---

32 Quoted in **Moulton and Milligan**, *Vocabulary of the Greek New Testament* (Peabody: Hendrikson Publishers, 1997).

substitute for our deserved punishment) and bearing the full curse of God on sin, that it is correctly understood as a propitiatory sacrifice. When Hebrews 2:17 alerts us to the important fact that he made 'propitiation for the sins of the people' (ESV), and Paul stresses that God sent him to be 'a propitiation by his blood' (Romans 3:25 ESV), everything that we have already discovered of the meaning of sacrifice in both Old and New Testaments is enshrined in that one word. By his death Jesus identified himself with the human race and offered to the Father a perfect sacrifice on behalf of those he would call his own. He carried their sin, guilt and punishment on the cross—as if they were his own—and this satisfied the just demand of a holy God that sin must receive due punishment.

It is in this sense that Christ pays the 'ransom' to set the prisoners free. The word ransom appears on only two occasions in the New Testament (Mark 10:45 and 1 Timothy 2:6), though redemption is a little more common. For example, redemption came by Christ Jesus (Romans 3:23) and this was 'through his blood' (Ephesians 1:7; Colossians 1:13; Hebrews 9:12). The price of our freedom was the death of the Son of God as the perfect Man, without a stain of sin. Redemption and propitiation are two parts of the same gain: Christ satisfied the demands of the justice of God by bearing the wrath due against sin. This was the price to be paid in order for the guilty to go free.

The propitiatory sacrifice of Christ was in every respect an act of unmerited love on the part of God. Paul insisted on this: 'God demonstrates his own love for us in this: While we were still sinners, Christ died for us' (Romans 5:8). And so did John:

In this the love of God was made manifest among us, that God sent his only Son into the world, so that we might live through him. In this is love, not that we have loved God but that he loved us and sent his Son to be the propitiation for our sins (1 John 4:9–10 ESV).

A willing sacrifice of love

This understanding of the atonement has been more recently caricatured as some form of cruel child abuse by which a father punishes his own son for sins he did not commit and which the father knew full well that he did not commit.[33] Such a response to propitiation falls on three counts.

First, it does not take into account the whole plan of the sacrificial system revealed by God under the Old Covenant. By the same argument, was the slaughter of thousands of animals an example of divine animal cruelty?

Secondly, it does not allow for the weight of Scripture that we have already surveyed which reveals Christ fulfilling the propitiatory sacrifices of the Old Covenant and thus falling under the punishment and curse of the Father.

But thirdly, such a view overlooks the perfect harmony of the Father and Son in the plan of salvation.

Christ did not die as an unwilling sacrifice under the stern demands of a relentlessly angry God. The relationship between the Father and the Son was a perfect union of thought and purpose; the repeated claims of Jesus make this clear:

I and the Father are one (John 10:30).

My food is to do the will of him who sent me and to finish his work (John 4:34).

I have come down from heaven not to do my will but to do the will of him who sent me. And this is the will of him who sent me, that I shall lose none of all that he has given me, but raise them up at the last day. For my Father's will is that everyone who looks to the Son and believes in him shall have eternal life, and I will raise him up at the last day (John 6:38–40).

His disciples remembered that it is written: 'Zeal for your house will consume me.' (John 2:17).

---

33 Brian McLaren places this phrase on the lips of one of his fictional characters to dismiss penal substitution: 'That just sounds like one more injustice in the cosmic equation. It sounds like divine child abuse.' Quoted in **Brian D. McLaren,** *The Story We Find Ourselves In* (San Francisco: Jossey Bass Wiley, 2003), p. 102). Chalke and Mann have more recently followed this line.

His was a willing obedience to the eternal plan of salvation. It was costly and agonising, but never unwilling. When he prayed more than once in the Garden 'My Father, if it is possible, may this cup be taken from me. Yet not as I will, but as you will' (Matthew 26:39), he revealed the awfulness of what lay ahead. But it was always as much his own plan as that of the Father.

This cannot be stressed too much. When confronting the Jewish leaders with the true purpose of his mission he claimed: 'The reason my Father loves me is that I lay down my life—only to take it up again. No-one takes it from me, but I lay it down of my own accord. I have authority to lay it down and authority to take it up again. This command I received from my Father' (John 10:17–18). That is hardly a hint of divine child abuse.

At the baptism of Jesus: a voice from heaven said, 'This is my Son, whom I love; with him I am well pleased.' (Matthew 3:17). And again on the mount of transfiguration, the Father declared: 'This is my Son, whom I love; with him I am well pleased. Listen to him!' (Matthew 17:5).

When Peter described the salvation of Christians as 'chosen according to the foreknowledge of God the Father, through the sanctifying work of the Spirit, for obedience to Jesus Christ and sprinkling by his blood' (1 Peter 1:2), he was declaring, in the shortest possible form, the plan of salvation in the councils of eternity; it was a perfect harmony between the Triune Godhead in which each person played his willing role in the salvation of lost sinners. To suggest anything else is a disastrous misunderstanding of the meaning of the cross. The Son came willingly, not grudgingly, and the Father never ceased to love his Son even at the moment when he 'became sin for us'.

However, God had to show the seriousness of sin and at the same time provide a way of forgiveness and reconciliation in a manner that was consistent with his justice. This could be accomplished in no clearer or more forceful way than by the sacrifice of his Son as a substitute in place of sinners. Paul's phrase in Romans 8:32 that God 'did not spare his own Son, but gave him up for us all', contains more than a hint that although the sacrifice of Christ was a willing act by both the Father and Son, it was nevertheless costly—a reluctant willingness is perhaps the best way that we can describe it. It was the only just way, but an incredibly costly way.

The resurrection and the atonement

When Paul set out those matters of primary importance in 1 Corinthians 15:3–4, he did not stop at 'Christ died for our sins according to the Scriptures'. He continued with the claim that 'he was buried, that he was raised on the third day according to the Scriptures.' Similarly, when Paul pressed home the significance of the death of Christ on our behalf so that we who died with him should no longer live for ourselves but for him, he added 'who died for them and was raised again' (2 Corinthians 5:15).

We said earlier that not until he had risen from the dead could Jesus persuade his disciples from 'all the Scriptures' of the true significance of the recent events. From those Scriptures he could now convince them of two great facts: that the Christ had 'to suffer … and then enter his glory' (Luke 24:26).

The atonement was incomplete without the resurrection for, according to Paul, if there is no resurrection then there is no forgiveness and no gospel—we are hopelessly lost (1 Corinthians 15:17–19). That claim alone is sufficient to demonstrate that the cross and the resurrection are both inextricably bound together for the work of salvation.

This is nowhere more clearly stated than in the single expression of Paul that 'He was delivered over to death for our sins and was raised to life for our justification' (Romans 4:25). This means more than that by his resurrection power we can be born again (Romans 5:10) and brought into a 'living hope' (1 Peter 1:3). 'Raised for our justification' implies that without the resurrection, the cross would not have achieved the ultimate purpose of reconciling the sinner to God. Justification is the act by which the Father declares us free from guilt and its eternal consequences. If the price was paid on the cross, the stamp of the Father's approval was evident in the resurrection.

Constantly Paul emphasised the fact that Christ was 'raised from the dead through the glory of the Father' (Romans 6:4 and compare 2 Corinthians 4:14; Galatians 1:1; Ephesians 1:20; Colossians 2:12; 1 Thessalonians 1:10). The 'cry of dereliction' at the cross: 'My God, my God why have you forsaken me?'(Matthew 27:46) received its final and confirming response from the Father when he raised his Son from the dead. Certainly it was not possible for death to hold him (Acts 2:24), but it was the Father's *imprimatur* on all that his Son had accomplished by his life and death. It was the Father's 'Amen' to the penal substitution of the cross.

However, the resurrection was not only objective proof that all has been accomplished for our salvation, it was the means by which we also could be 'made alive' in Christ, not just in the future (1 Corinthians 15:22), but now, in the present (Ephesians 2:5). By his death *and* resurrection Christ, the last Adam, can reverse the spiritual death that passed from the first Adam to the human race, and can set us free from slavery to sin, Satan and the fear of death: 'our old self was crucified with him so that the body of sin might be done away with, that we should no longer be slaves to sin—because anyone who has died has been freed from sin' (Romans 6:6–7).

The resurrection of Jesus is proof that the works of the devil have been destroyed and that captivity has been taken captive. We await only the day when he returns in power and glory in order to put all his enemies under his feet and hand over the kingdom to the Father (1 Corinthians 15:24–28). Equally, the whole of creation is anticipating the liberation that was won at the cross and in the empty tomb, and that will be realised at the return of Christ in glory (Romans 8:17,19).

Meanwhile, because of his resurrection, the benefits of the cross can be effective for us in heaven: 'Because Jesus lives for ever, he has a permanent priesthood. Therefore he is able to save completely those who come to God through him, because he always lives to intercede for them' (Hebrews 7:24).

PART TWO
THE ATONEMENT IN CHURCH HISTORY

The atonement in the Early Church

'O sweetest exchange! O unfathomable accomplishment! O unexpected blessings!'[1]

Despite what some have claimed, there is a significant amount of teaching from the early church period in which the death of Christ is described as both penal and substitutionary. This underlies much of what the early Christian Fathers wrote, and it was certainly not rejected or repudiated by those who remained in the mainstream of Christian orthodoxy. Their writings are frequently pastorally motivated, dealing with issues that troubled their churches, or questions as to how the gospel was to be related to the social and cultural context. The lack of extensive discussion in some of the writings of the early Christian leaders does not imply that penal substitution was an insignificant doctrine to them, but rather that it does not appear to have been a particularly controversial matter.

POLYCARP
One very significant figure in the early church was Polycarp, the Bishop of Smyrna, who endured a heroic martyrdom for his faith in the middle of the second century, when he was well over eighty years old. As a young man he knew the apostle John, and met with other eyewitnesses of the life of

---

1 'Epistle to Diognetus', in *Ancient Christian Writers*, Vol. VI, **trans. J.A. Kleist** (London: Longmans, 1948), IX, 2–6, p. 143.

Christ. He is therefore an important figure in maintaining the tradition of apostolic teaching. In his letter to the Philippians he used the language of substitution to describe how he understands the atonement. Christ was willing to suffer for our sins, which is the strong root of our faith; as he died he 'took up our sins in his own body upon the tree, who did no sin, neither was guile found in his mouth, but for our sakes He endured all things, that we might live in Him'.[2]

JUSTIN MARTYR

As the church responded to its commission to proclaim the gospel, it was first shared with Jewish people, often in a local synagogue. Sometimes Christian preachers were positively received, but frequently their message was viewed as controversial, especially when it concerned the death of Christ upon the cross. During the second century AD, the issue remained pressing. One Christian who particularly sought to express Christianity in a way that could be readily understood by outsiders to the faith was Justin, a Christian apologist (one who defends the faith publicly). Born around AD 100, he was martyred for his faith around 165, and is usually referred to as Justin Martyr. Justin wrote 'apologies' for the Christian faith that were addressed to pagan readers; his *Dialogue with Trypho* is presented in the form of a debate with a learned Jew, whose conversion Justin longed for.

It was no easy task, however, for a major issue that Trypho could not accept was the death of Christ, the Messiah, upon a cross: 'Whether Christ should be so shamefully crucified, this we are in doubt about. For whosoever is crucified is said in the law to be accursed, so that I am exceedingly incredulous on this point.' Justin answered that it was necessary for Christ to be 'dishonoured and scourged, and reckoned among the transgressors', and to do this 'on account of the sins of the people'. To do this he needed to identify with fallen humanity, and take upon himself not only their sins, but also the 'curse', the judgement, that those sins

---

2 **Polycarp,** *Letter to Philippians, Section 8,* in **J.B. Lightfoot,** *Apostolic Fathers* (London: Macmillan, 1890), p. 180.

attracted. Justin therefore argued that God's plan was for Christ, 'for the whole human family, to take upon Him the curses of us all, knowing that, after He had been crucified and was dead, He would raise Him up.' Justin was absolutely certain that this was a real, and necessary, act of substitution: he stressed that it was on 'behalf of the human family'. Arguing from Isaiah, and particularly Psalm 22, he emphasised that God 'wished His Son really to undergo such sufferings for our sakes.' The substitutionary nature of Christ's death was affirmed by reference to the Passover: 'And as the blood of the Passover saved those who were in Egypt, so also the blood of Christ will deliver from death those who have believed.'[3] Justin had no doubt that the cross involved Christ identifying with, and bearing, the curse on humans for their sin—the just punishment of God. Whether Trypho, or other Jews, were converted through Justin's argument is not recorded.

THE EPISTLE TO DIOGNETUS
Another mid-second century apologist was the writer of the Epistle to Diognetus. The author's name is unknown, but in the letter the writer defended Christians against the false charges of their persecutors, and set out what is so special about Christianity. The warmth of the letter, as it explained the atonement, is remarkable: 'When the cup of our iniquities was filled, and it had become perfectly clear that their wages—the punishment of death—had to be expected, then the season arrived during which God determined to reveal henceforth His goodness and power.' The writer is overwhelmed at the grace of God in the provision of a substitute for sinners: 'No, He did not hate us, or discard us, or remember our wrongs; He exercised forbearance and long-suffering! In mercy, of His own accord, He lifted up the burden of our sins! Of His own accord *He gave us His own Son* as a ransom for us—the Saint for sinners, the Guiltless for the

---

3 **Justin Martyr,** *Dialogue With Trypho the Jew*, Chapters 89, 95, 103, 111, in **A. Roberts and J. Donaldson (eds),** *Ante-Nicene Fathers* (Edinburgh: 1867. Reprinted Grand Rapids: Eerdmans, 1973), Vol. I, pp. 244–51. It is unclear if the 'dialogue' actually took place, or whether it was a literary form used by Justin to present his arguments.

guilty, *the Innocent for the wicked*, the Incorruptible for the corruptible, the Immortal for the mortal! Indeed, what else could have covered our sins but His holiness?' The writer spelled out the great exchange—how what was the sinner's in terms of punishment and death became Christ's: 'O sweetest exchange! O unfathomable accomplishment! O unexpected blessings—the sinfulness of many is buried in One who is holy, the holiness of One justifies the many who are sinners!'[4]

At the heart of this act is the amazing love of God.

IRENAEUS

When in AD 177 a wave of persecution led to the death of the elderly bishop Pothinus in Lyons, he was succeeded by Irenaeus who, as a young man, had heard Polycarp preach. Through him, Irenaeus was able to maintain a continuity with apostolic preaching, a point he was anxious to emphasise. Irenaeus is famous for his teaching of 'recapitulation', showing how the obedience of Jesus Christ as the second Adam put right each aspect of the disobedience of the first Adam: 'Wherefore he also passed through every stage of life, restoring all to communion with God.'[5] This work culminated at the cross where, by obedience to death at the tree of Calvary, Jesus Christ undid the disobedience of Adam at the tree in the Garden of Eden.[6] In order for 'recapitulation' to be effectual, however, Christ had by nature to be both God and Man. Because he is both, he is an utterly sufficient Saviour: 'So by obedience, whereby He obeyed unto death, hanging on the tree, He undid the old disobedience wrought in the tree.' Irenaeus therefore stressed both the physical reality of the death of Jesus, and its spiritual reality as a work of substitution, whereby he bears the debt in the place of the sinner, and the demands of God's justice are met. As he showed by quoting Isaiah:

---

4 'Epistle to Diognetus' in *Ancient Christian Writers*, trans. **J.A. Kleist** (London: Longmans, 1948), Vol. VI, IX , 2–6 [Italics are as found in the translation].

5 **Irenaeus,** III, 19, 6, in J. Stevenson (ed.) *A New Eusebius* (London: SPCK, 1987), p. 119.

6 **Irenaeus,** *Proof of Apostolic Preaching*, Section 34 (London: Longman, Green and Co. 1952), p. 69.

'He beareth our sins, and for our sake suffereth pains, and we esteemed him to be in pains and in bruises and in torments. But he was wounded because of our iniquities, and was tormented because of our sins ... judgement has been taken *on* some, and they have in it the torments of their perdition; but *off* others and they are thereby saved.'[7]

THE THREAT FROM MARCION

When Marcion arrived in Rome just before 140 he brought teaching that was very damaging to the church. He drew a distinction between Old and New Testament, between the god of the Old Testament, and the Father of the Lord Jesus Christ. Marcion argued that the god of the Old Testament was an inferior being, who was to be rejected as a god of law, and of justice and punishment. In contrast the God revealed in the New Testament is one of love, and grace. Marcion produced his own canon of New Testament Scripture, containing those texts which he believed supported his teaching: the Gospel of Luke, ten of Paul's epistles, but not the pastoral epistles or Hebrews. Even from these, passages that did not agree with his teachings were cut out, leaving a 'Bible' that emphasised love and grace. Marcion's work was roundly condemned by leaders of orthodox Christianity, but he attracted a range of followers, and sympathetic churches sprang up. His work helped challenge orthodox Christianity to address the issue of the canon of New Testament Scripture, and to set out what the church was to teach about creation, the Fall, and redemption. Marcion and his churches have long gone, but the challenge of Marcionite thinking remains today, with a continued tendency amongst some to emphasise the love of God to the exclusion of all else, especially sin and the justice and judgement of God, and all too often a discontinuity is drawn between the New and the Old Testaments.

TERTULLIAN

One of those who strongly opposed Marcion's teaching was the sharp-

---

7 **Irenaeus,** *Apostolic Preaching*, Section 68–69, pp.92–93 [Italics are as found in the translation].

thinking North African Christian writer Tertullian (c. 160/170—c. 215/220). He had no doubt that the death of Christ was 'the whole world's only hope.' The events of Calvary were Christ's supreme work, for he 'overcame death by His suffering on the cross, and thence reigned.'[8] As with earlier writers, he emphasised the Son of God's role as a substitute who bore the curse for sinners:

God spared not his own Son for you, that he might be a curse for us ... being numbered with the transgressors, [he] was delivered up to death, nay the death of the cross.[9]

ORIGEN

Amongst the theologians of the early church, one of the most significant was Origen (c. 185–c. 254). He was a brilliant, devoted, and controversial figure. His main work was the twenty-eight years he spent as head of the catechetical school in Alexandria, and he later established a similar school in Caesarea. Origen is well-known for discussing how the work of Christ was one of ransom, based on Mark 10:45. Humans were held captive until the coming of the Son of God, who by paying the ransom price brings redemption. However, Origen's understanding of 'ransom' causes significant theological problems. He believed that humanity was held captive by the devil, who accepted Christ's sinless life as the ransom price which God was obliged to pay. But the devil miscalculated in accepting this bargain, was overwhelmed by the Son of God's divine goodness, and had to let both Christ and the captives go free. This view, which was developed by a number of theologians in the early and medieval church, including Peter Lombard, attributes too much power to the devil by suggesting that he had rights over humanity, and that God was reduced to bargaining with him. Portraying the devil as being deceived into defeat also has the demerit of attributing a fraudulent action to God.

---

8 **Tertullian,** *On the Flesh.* v; and *Five Books Against Marcion* Book III, xix, in *Ante-Nicene Fathers* (1885, repr. 1978), Vol. III., pp.525, 337.

9 **Tertullian,** *De fugâ in persecutione,* in *Ante-Nicene Fathers,* (1885, repr. 1979), Vol. IV, p. 123.

Nonetheless, it would be a great mistake to think that this was all that Origen had to say about the atonement. Origen was an early biblical commentator, and in dealing with Scripture he came across passages that explain the death of Christ in both substitutionary and penal terms. In his commentary on John's Gospel he discussed how Jesus is 'the Lamb of God, who takes away the sin of the world.' Origen linked this verse to John's first epistle, and to other Scriptures: 'He is a propitiation for our sins, and similarly Paul says He is a propitiation: "Whom God set forth as a propitiation through faith in His blood, on account of forgiveness of the forepast sins, in the forbearance of God".' Origen believed this work of propitiation was prefigured at the heart of the Old Testament sacrificial system: 'There was a type in the inmost part of the temple, the Holy of Holies, namely, the golden mercy seat placed between the two cherubim.'[10]

Origen also demonstrated the link between the biblical picture of Christ's death as being a ransom for sinners and this teaching of propitiation. The 'many wonderful things' he believes the Epistle to the Romans teaches about the cross, begin with the fact that Christ ransomed 'those who were held captive by sin'; then Origen found 'something even more sublime ... "God put him forward as an expiation on behalf of men."' His argument reached a culmination when he considered Romans 3:26:

In the most recent times, God has manifested his righteousness and given Christ to be our redemption. He has made him our propitiator ... for God is just, and therefore could not justify the unjust. Therefore he required the intervention of a propitiator, so that by having faith in him those who could not be justified by their own works might be justified.

To Origen, therefore, the cross is the place where God's justice is satisfied. Christ has accomplished a work of propitiation that turns away judgement. Thus, 'At the present time ... God's righteousness is revealed for our justification.' However, this will not always remain the case: 'When the day of judgement comes, it [God's righteousness] will be revealed for

---

10 Origen, *Commentary on John's Gospel,* Book I, 23, and Book I, 38, in *Ante-Nicene Fathers,* Vol. IV. pp. 309, 317.

retribution.' Ransom, expiation, and propitiation are drawn together, with propitiation absolutely pivotal: the judgement of God for unrighteousness is borne by another, Jesus Christ. His death deals with sin; this ransoms the believer from captivity.[11]

In Origen's thinking, Christ's work of propitiation was closely linked to the resurrection and ascension. He quoted from 1 John 2:1–2, and then explained:

'We have an advocate with the Father, Jesus Christ the righteous: and He is the propitiation for our sins, and not only for ours only, but for those of the whole world.' Since He is the Saviour of all men, especially of them that believe, who blotted out the written bond that was against us by His own blood, so that not even a trace of our blotted-out sins might still be found, and nailed it to His cross; who having put off from Himself the principalities and powers, made a show of them openly, triumphing over them by His cross.[12]

The Scripture language of 'victory', taken up by later theologians in writing of the cross, is again firmly connected to the propitiatory work of Christ, and his ongoing intercession at the right hand of the Father. Origen, as a biblical commentator, drew on the wide range of images found within Scripture for understanding the atonement, but he placed propitiation at their heart. In doing this he was no more than being faithful to what he found in Scripture.

ALEXANDER AND ATHANASIUS
Alexandria, where Origen served as head of the catechetical school, was the scene of one of the most important theological debates in the history of the church early in the fourth century. A highly popular presbyter called Arius began to promote a view that God the Son was not an eternal being, but that

---

11 **Origen,** *Commentary on Romans*, Romans 3:25–26, in *Ancient Commentary on Scripture: The New Testament, VI, Romans,* **ed. G. Bray** (Downers Grove, Illinois: IVP, 1998), pp. 101–103.

12 **Origen,** *Commentary on John*, Book VI. 37, p. 378.

he was created by the Father. Arius believed that the Son was not co-eternal with the Father, and was therefore inferior to him. Arius was a fine communicator, who had influential friends, and his teaching began to spread rapidly. His teaching was condemned at the Council of Nicea in AD 325, where the deity of Christ was affirmed. The controversy raised issues not only about the nature of God, but also about Scripture and its interpretation, and about salvation. Bishop Alexander of Alexandria argued strongly that only one who was truly the incarnate God, not one who is inferior to God, could accomplish salvation: 'In the cause of redemption to give life for life, blood for blood, to undergo death for death.' The death of Christ discharged the debt, which was borne as a substitute for others: 'One submitted himself to judgement, and many thousands were absolved.'[13]

Arianism continued to have a major impact on the church in the fourth century. The most formidable opponent of Arianism in the church in the Eastern Mediterranean area was Athanasius (c. 296–373), who succeeded Alexander as bishop of Alexandria. He realised that the very Godhead, and therefore the way of salvation, was at stake in the controversy. The doctrine of the incarnation, and the doctrine of the atonement, were inseparably linked: how could one who was not God, reconcile us to God? Athanasius dealt firmly with those who suggested that repentance alone could deal with the problem of sin. First, he showed that the view conflicts with Scripture. Secondly, he asserted that repentance would not satisfy what is due to God: because of sin, people are held in the grip of the power of death, and mere repentance is not enough to deliver us from this grip or fulfil the binding demands of the law. Only the Word, by whom all things were made, was able to satisfy what is due to the Father not only by interceding, but also by suffering a substitutionary death for sinners: 'But since the debt owed by all men still had to be paid ... he now on behalf of all men offered the sacrifice and surrendered his own temple to death on behalf of all.' In dying this death Christ willingly 'became accursed.'[14]

---

13 **Alexander,** *On the Soul and Body,* Section 7, in *Ante-Nicene Fathers,* Vol. VI, p. 583. xiv. pp. 362, 356.

14 **Athanasius,** *De Incarnatione,* IX, 1, 24, in *Oxford Early Christian Texts: Athanasius* (Oxford: Clarendon, 1971), pp. 183, 195.

Athanasius was clear that in this cursed death Christ bore the punishment due against sin. This is how he understood the request 'made on humanity's behalf' in Psalm 72:1, '"Give to the King thy judgement, O God" asking that the judgement of death which hung over us may be delivered to the Son, and also that he may then, by dying for us, abolish it for us in himself. This is what he signified, saying himself, in the eighty-eighth Psalm "Thine indignation lieth hard upon me." For he bore the indignation which lay upon us.'[15]

In the light of those who have argued that penal substitution is a recent doctrine in the history of the church, Athanasius in the fourth century provides a firm and explicit statement of the fact that the death of Christ was necessary to satisfy the just demands of the law and the justice of God, and that he bore the curse and punishment of God against sin. Athanasius also strongly showed that to attack the doctrine of the incarnation, is to undermine the teaching of the church on salvation.

CYRIL AND EUSEBIUS

The same point is made by Cyril, Bishop of Jerusalem (c. 310–386). In the thirteenth of his *Catecheses*, Cyril showed how, through the death of Christ, God maintains the justice of his sentence against sin, and yet shows free grace: 'Shall not Jesus bring to naught God's wrath against men, by— not slaying another, but—delivering up himself as a ransom in exchange.'[16]

Eusebius of Caesarea (c. 265–c. 339), renowned as the 'Father of Church History', wrote widely on a range of other topics. In his *Demonstratio Evangelica* he showed how Christianity can be proved from the Old Testament. Drawing attention to Isaiah 53, Eusebius depicted the atonement of Christ as a work of substitution, on behalf of sinners:

[He] was chastised on our behalf, and suffered a penalty He did not owe, but which we owed because of the multitude of our sins; and so He became the cause of the

---

15 **Athanasius,** *Illud 'Omnia': On Luke 10, 22 (Matthew 11:27)*, Section 2, in *Nicene and Post-Nicene Fathers*, 2nd *series*, Vol IV, (Grand Rapids: repr. Eerdmans, 1978), p. 88.

16 **Cyril of Jerusalem,** *Catecheses*, XIII, 2, quoted in **J. Dimock,** *The Doctrine of the Death of Christ* (London: Elliot Stock, n.d.), p. 99.

forgiveness of our sins, because He received death for us, and transferred to Himself the scourging, the insults, and the dishonour, which were due to us, and drew down on himself the apportioned curse, being made a curse for us. And what is that but the price of our souls.[17]

Eusebius shows how the ideas of ransom and bearing punishment are inextricably linked—the blood of Christ not only pays the ransom price to deliver the sinner from bondage, it is also an act of propitiation, dealing with the just demands of God.

AUGUSTINE OF HIPPO

Augustine (354–430) of Hippo, in North Africa, was converted later in life, after a long spiritual search that saw him explore a variety of philosophical systems. His struggles with a sense of sin and guilt over his pre-Christian life made his teaching on the atonement of particular relevance for his own spiritual battles. He was to become the dominant theologian of his era. As a great biblical preacher, and expositor, Augustine dealt thoroughly with Scripture passages that addressed this theme, although he offered no systematic discussion of the topic. Commenting on Romans 2:5 he showed how sin brings upon the sinner the wrath of God and: 'Every time Paul speaks of the wrath of God, he means it in the sense of punishment.' Although sin incurs the curse, God in Christ has acted as a substitute for sinners: 'On whose behalf, as no one doubts, the Lord himself was called "sin", because "he bore our sins" (cf John 1:29; 1 Peter 2:24), and "made sin for us" (cf 2 Corinthians 5:21).' God is 'steadfast in divine justice,' and sin attracts a 'spiritual and eternal penalty,' but from this penalty, those who repent are spared, because it has been paid by another.[18]

---

17 Eusebius, *Demonstratio Evangelica*, x, 1,
www.tertullian.org/fathers/eusebius_de_12_book10.htm., quoted by Garry Williams, 'Justice, Law and Guilt', Evangelical Alliance Symposium, London School of Theology, 8 July 2005.

18 Augustine, 'Propositions from the Epistle to the Romans', in *Augustine on Romans: Propositions from the Epistle to the Romans; Unfinished Commentary on the Epistle to the Romans*, **ed. P.F. Landes** (Chico, California: Scholars Press, 1982), pp. 5, 13, 63.

Some of Augustine's works were written against Manichæanism—a religious system which had fascinated him early in his life. Again he reverted to the issue of how Jesus Christ was hanged on a tree, and therefore under God's curse. What does this death mean? Referring to Romans 6, he explained:

Death is the effect of the curse; and all sin is cursed, whether it means the action which merits punishment, or the punishment which follows. Christ, though guiltless, took our punishment, that He might cancel our guilt, and do away with our punishment.

Augustine again stressed that the death of Christ was both substitutionary and penal: 'As He died in the flesh which He took in bearing our punishment, so also, while ever blessed in His own righteousness, He was cursed for our offences, in the death which He suffered in bearing our punishment.'[19]

JOHN CHRYSOSTOM

Another great preacher of the fourth century was John Chrysostom (c. 344/354–407). He made his reputation as a preacher in the cathedral at Antioch, and was later remembered as *chrysostomos*, which means 'golden mouthed'. He preached in a plain, practical, lively and earnest style. He thought deeply about 2 Corinthians 5:21, and the mystery of how the One who knew no sin, could become sin. The death of Jesus Christ was no mere death, 'For this thing carried with it not only punishment, but also disgrace.' He urged his congregation to ponder the wonder of this, and was overwhelmed with his theme: 'What words, what thought shall be adequate to realise these things.' Chrysostom struggled to express the awesome truth that, 'God allowed his Son to suffer as if a condemned sinner, so that we might be delivered from the penalty of our sins. This is God's righteousness, that we are not justified by works ... but by grace in which case all our sin is removed.'

---

19 Augustine, Contra Faustum, Book XIV, 4, 6, in *Nicene and Post-Nicene Fathers,* Vol. IV, **ed. P. Schaff** (reprinted Grand Rapids: 1979), pp. 208–09.

Chrysostom emphasised how such a subject leads to worship, and offers a response to those who claim that teaching on penal substitution does not inspire a response to better moral conduct. Far from this, he was convinced that it promoted a hatred of sin, and a love for holiness: as he dramatically expressed it—'We ought to take vengeance on ourselves, who have been so ungrateful towards our benefactor.' The believer should 'groan bitterly for the provocations we have offered our Benefactor', and to have a holy horror of sin: 'Let us not only be afraid of, but also flee from it, and strive to please God continually; for this is the kingdom, this is life ... this is ten thousand goods.'[20]

The sermons and writings of preachers and theologians in the first centuries of the Christian church reflect the rich variety of ways in which the Bible speaks about the cross. Clearly, and consistently, they speak of how the death of Christ was substitutionary in character, and how it involved bearing the penalty, or curse, justly due for the sinfulness of mankind. Their understanding of the work of the cross was inseparable from their understanding of the person who died on the cross. The ultimate purpose of the incarnation was Calvary, as the theologians assembled at the Council of Chalcedon affirmed in 451, God the Son took flesh, 'for us and our salvation.'[21] This salvation, the awesome transaction, the 'sweet exchange' of the atonement, could only have been accomplished by the life, death and resurrection of the One who was truly God, and truly Man. Only if Christ is God incarnate can we be certain of the fruits of his atoning sacrifice, that God's justice has been eternally satisfied, that the penalty of sin has been paid, and that the believer has been reconciled, and has peace, with God.

20 **John Chrysostom,** 'Homilies on the Epistles of Paul to the Corinthians', in *Nicene and Post-Nicene Fathers*, Vol XII, v–vi, pp.334–335.

21 The Chalcedonian Definition of the Faith, Section 4.

The atonement in the Medieval Period

'Mine was the transgression, but thine the deadly pain.'[1]

arly Christian theologians laid a foundation upon which later teachers built. They emphasised that the cross was the place of the curse, and that the curse that Jesus Christ bore was the penalty for sin, which was borne as a substitute in the place of sinners. The medieval period was certainly one in which this Christian teaching developed. However, as the church moved out of the clearly post-biblical period, theologians attempted to express their ideas in a manner suitable to medieval culture. There were times when culture, and wider philosophical environment, moulded the way theologians spoke about the atonement more strongly than the foundational biblical material. A variety of understandings of the atonement were put forward in the medieval period, some of which proved controversial, and attracted opposition from leading theologians of the time. The legacy left by thinking about the cross in the medieval period proved a mixed one. However, the pattern of teaching set in the early church was never forgotten.

GREGORY THE GREAT

The chief architect of the medieval Roman Catholic papal bureaucracy was Gregory the Great (540–604), a noted theologian, particularly in the field of pastoral care. In his *Moralia in Jobum* ('Book of Morals'—a commentary on Job), he set out a developed statement of the atonement as a work of penal substitution:

Guilt can be extinguished only by a penal offering to justice … But how could a man, himself stained with sin, be an offering for sin? Hence a sinless man must be offered.

---

1 From the hymn 'O sacred head once wounded', attributed to **Bernard of Clairvaux.**

But what man descending in the ordinary course would be free of sin? Hence the Son of God must be born of a virgin, and become a man for us. He assumed our nature without our corruption. He made himself a sacrifice for us, and set forth for sinners his own body—a victim without sin, and able both to die by virtue of its humanity, and to cleanse the guilty upon grounds of justice.[2]

JOHN OF DAMASCUS

The writings of John of Damascus, who died in 750, are still afforded a very high status in the Eastern churches. John's writings reveal an understanding of the death of Christ that is both substitutionary and penal: 'He who assumed death for us, died, and offered himself a sacrifice to the Father; for we had committed wrong towards him, and it was necessary for him to receive our ransom, and we thus be delivered from condemnation.'[3]

ANSELM

A major contribution to thinking about the atonement in the Western church came from Anselm. He certainly lived in troubled times, and his own life had its tempestuous moments. He was born in Italy around the year 1033, but after a quarrel with his father he left home and for several years wandered across Europe before settling in Normandy and becoming a monk. To this new role he settled, and progressed in his abbey to become prior, and then abbot. When he was sixty years old Anselm was appointed by the new Norman rulers of England as Archbishop of Canterbury, a post he held until his death sixteen years later.

In these unstable, troubled, and changing times, Anselm wrote much. He is famous for his profound arguments in favour of the existence of God, making faith central to understanding the truth about God: 'I do not seek to understand that I may believe, but I believe that I may understand.' Anselm wrote probably the first detailed attempt to explain the reason and necessity of the cross as the way of atonement. His *Cur Deus Homo?* ('Why God became Man?') was much shaped by the context in which he worked,

---

2 **Gregory,** *Moralia in Jobum,* quoted in **A.A. Hodge,** *The Atonement* (London: Nelson and Sons, 1868), pp. 261–62.

3 **John of Damascus,** *Expositio Fidei,* iii, 27, in **A.A. Hodge,** *Atonement,* p. 262.

where noble knights operated to codes of honour and chivalry. Feudal law dominated life, with a complex series of penalties and punishments for offences. Alongside these laws, the concept of 'satisfaction' developed: an injured person could in some way be compensated, without an exact reparation of what had been lost.

Anselm drew on these ideas when he wrote about the atonement. He began with the key issue that had dominated early church leaders in their debates with Jewish thinkers—why did God become Man? Even more troubling: Why did he take on the indignities of the human condition and suffer a tortured death on the cross? Why could God not have simply forgiven humans by a divine decree?

Anselm importantly rejected the view adopted by some early church thinkers, that Jesus died to pay a ransom to the devil, by showing that the devil is only a creature, and knows no concept of justice. To Anselm, sin was 'not to render his due to God.' Sin is an offence against the honour and greatness of God, to whom, as the infinite, Sovereign Creator and Redeemer, all honour is due. Even the smallest offence therefore requires infinite satisfaction: 'Anyone who does not give this honour to God takes away from God what belongs to Him, and dishonours Him; and this is sin.'[4]

Suppose two labourers get into a fight, and hit each other, because they are of equal social status, and exchange equal blows, satisfaction could be brought by them pardoning each other. But what if a labourer strikes the king? How much greater the offence? Then, at the ultimate level of gravity, what of the offence of sinning against God? So, Anselm argued that if God merely forgave sin it would be unbecoming of him; it would be inconsistent with his character and dignity.[5] Anselm therefore concluded, 'It is necessary that either satisfaction or punishment must follow all sin.'[6] Because of the greatness of God's character, only one who is of the status of God can make such satisfaction. The problem is that it is humans who need to make the satisfaction, *they* are the offenders, not God. The only resolution to this

---

4 **Anselm,** *Cur Deus Homo* (London: Griffith, Farran, Okeden and Welsh edition. n.d.). Book I, Chapter 11.

5 *Cur Deus Homo,* I, 12.

6 *Cur Deus Homo,* I, 15.

dilemma is found in Jesus. As both God and Man, he is able to offer satisfaction, which deals with the needs both of God and of the human race: 'The life of this man was so ineffable, so beyond all price, that it would suffice to atone for what was due for all the sins of the world, and for infinitely more.'[7]

Anselm did not discuss all the aspects of the saving work of Jesus Christ, but he focused on why the incarnation and the cross were necessary. He rightly stressed how serious sin is, and how Jesus offers satisfaction, so that God's people can be spared from the punishment that was due to them. Yet, for Anselm the choice faced by God is punishment, or satisfaction, for sins. Because Jesus, by his life and death, satisfied the honour of God, merit is bestowed on him, which he, in turn, bestows on humans. Therefore, he did not argue that Jesus Christ bore the punishment, the curse, rightly due for sin—that did not prove necessary because satisfaction was offered. Anselm's treatment of the atonement, helpful as aspects of it are, leaves a number of difficulties.

The word 'satisfaction' is not used in scripture to refer to the work of Christ on the cross. Anselm said little about the justice of God, or the place of the resurrection, in the atonement. Anselm also said little about the love and grace of God in discussing the cross. In his presentation, what motivates God is not a loving desire to redeem sinners, but that his honour and dignity are satisfied. Others were later to build upon his teaching, but in itself Anselm's is an inadequate presentation of biblical teaching on the atonement. Perhaps he was aware of this, for when giving pastoral counsel to a dying believer who was troubled by his sense of sinfulness and fearful of the judgement of God, Anselm reverted to the more traditional language of penal substitution. He counselled the troubled soul to cry to God: '"Lord, I place the death of your Lord Jesus Christ between me and Thy judgement: in no other way do I contend with Thee" ... If He shall say that He is angry with thee, say, "Lord, I place the death of our Lord Jesus Christ between me and Thy anger."'[8]

---

7 *Cur Deus Homo*, II, 17.

8 Quoted in **H.D. McDonald,** *The Atonement of the Death of Christ in Faith, Revelation, and History* (Grand Rapids: Baker Books, 1985), p. 173.

PETER ABELARD

Another significant theological thinker of the medieval period was Peter Abelard, but he was a flawed genius. The story of his love affair with his beautiful, and equally brilliant, pupil Heloise is one of the tragic love stories of history. Born a little after Anselm in Brittany in 1079, Abelard studied in Paris under leading thinkers of his day, but he grew frustrated at their approach, and set himself up as a rival teacher. This made him popular with his pupils, but not with other academics. He was brilliant, and he knew it. But a fall was just around the corner. When he began to tutor the niece of his patron, the beautiful teenage girl Heloise, he fell deeply in love with her. It was a reckless love affair, for marriage would have ended his academic prospects; however, before long Heloise fell pregnant and a child was born. His patron, when he found out, was furious and Abelard secretly married Heloise to pacify him. But he was not pacified, and had his revenge. One night a mob of ruffians attacked Peter, beat him, and castrated him—his sexual offence would not be repeated. There was no happy ending to the love story. Abelard became a monk, and Heloise was left sad, bitter, and lonely.

Perhaps Abelard found it hard to reconcile himself to what he had done. He had discovered by personal experience that sin was 'guilt of the soul and contempt of God ... our perverted will by which we stand before God.'[9] When he began to write about Paul's teaching on the atonement in Romans, it is no surprise that he stressed the way the life and death of Christ, as a supreme demonstration of love, should inspire in us love and obedience to God. An understanding of the amazing act of the grace of God in the cross should liberate us from servitude to sin, and should bind the believer's heart to God in his love: 'Our hearts should be enkindled by such a gift of divine grace, and true love should not now shrink from enduring anything for him.'[10] This important reflection upon the cross was a profound challenge to Abelard's own errant behaviour.

However, Abelard criticised the approach of penal substitution: 'Indeed,

---

9 **Abelard,** *Exposition of Romans 11, 5*, quoted in **T. Gorringe,** *God's Just Vengeance* (Cambridge: Cambridge University Press. 1996), p. 112.

10 **Peter Abelard,** *Exposition of Romans (3:19–26). Appendix.*

how cruel and wicked it seems that anyone should demand the blood of an innocent person as the price for anything ... still less that God should consider the death of his Son so agreeable that by it he should be reconciled to the whole world!'[11] Instead, he made the love of God the be all and end all of God's nature, and suggested that God could have forgiven mankind without the death of Christ. In doing this, Abelard switched the purpose of the cross from being about what God has done in Christ for us, to a subjective matter relating to our response and feelings about the cross. Abelard's approach leaves difficulties which other theologians recognised. Unless something tangible was truly accomplished by Christ's death on the cross, other than it being an example to inspire us, what did it actually achieve? If it was not absolutely necessary for Christ to suffer and die in such a terrible way in order to bring forgiveness, why was another way not found?

Yet even a writer with such serious doubts over the teaching of penal substitution could not avoid drawing on such ideas when offering pastoral advice to his beloved Heloise, who had written to him declaring her continued love. He urged her instead to look to the cross of Christ: 'Are you not moved to tears or remorse by the only-begotten Son of God, who for you and all people, in his innocence was seized by impious men ... to die a horrible and accursed form of death ... he suffered truly for your salvation, on your behalf, of his own free will, and by his suffering he cures all sickness and removes all suffering.'[12] Similarly in his commentary on Romans he used expressions indicating that in his death Christ also bore the punishment for our sins. On Romans 4:25 Abelard observes that the death of Christ takes 'Our sins away, that is the punishment of sins, introducing us into Paradise at the price of his own death.' Again in Romans 8:3 he notes that Christ bore our sins 'by paying the penalty for them.'[13]

---

11 **Abelard,** *Exposition of Romans (3:19–26). Appendix.*

12 **Peter Abelard,** *The Letters of Heloise and Abelard* (Penguin: Harmondsworth, 1974), pp. 149–53.

13 **Abelard,** *Romans,* 4, 25; 8, 3. quoted in **H.D. McDonald,** *The Atonement of the Death of Christ: in Faith, Revelation, and History* (Grand Rapids: Baker, 1985), p. 177.

Abelard's chief understanding of the work of Christ upon the cross is a form of the 'moral influence theory' which has had other advocates in the medieval and later periods of the history of the church, and has again become popular recently, particularly for its overwhelming emphasis upon the love of God. Certainly it conveys one of the vital dimensions to the cross. What Jesus did should change our thinking, our morality, our self-giving. Love so amazing, so divine, does indeed demand our life, our soul, our all. The death of Jesus Christ supremely reveals the love of God, and leads the believer to love him more. However, the evidence of Scripture, and the teaching of the early church, shows that this is not all there is to say about the cross. The cross is more than simply an example of love.

BERNARD OF CLAIRVAUX

Another significant medieval figure was convinced that Peter Abelard had got it wrong. Bernard of Clairvaux was born near Dijon in 1090 to a noble family. In his early twenties he entered the abbey of Citeaux, the first of those established by the recently founded Cistercian order. After three years, Bernard was appointed to the post of abbot of the new monastery at Clairvaux, the place he became most popularly associated with. He is a complex figure, but a man of deep devotion, who could write:

Jesus the very thought of thee,
With sweetness fills my breast,
But sweeter far thy face to see,
And in thy presence rest.

Bernard argued strongly against Abelard's view that Christ lived and died 'for no other purpose than that he might teach man how to love by his words and example.' Bernard wished to stress the love of God, but also believed that the death of Christ had accomplished something before a just God, which was to save the believer from the consequences of sin: 'I was made a sinner by deriving my being from Adam ... Shall generation by a sinner be sufficient to condemn me and shall not the blood of Christ be sufficient to justify me? ... Such is the justice which man has obtained through the blood of the Redeemer.'[14] He went on to set out the atonement of Christ as being both penal and substitutionary:

If one died for all, then all were dead, that the satisfaction of one might be imputed to all, as he alone bore the sins of all; and now he who offended, and he who satisfied divine justice, are found the same, because the head and the body is one Christ.[15]

In the famous hymn attributed to him, 'O sacred head once wounded,' Bernard again focuses his thoughts upon the substitutionary death of Christ:

I read the wondrous story,
I joy to call thee mine
Thy grief and thy compassion
Were all for sinner's gain;
Mine, mine was the transgression,
But thine the deadly pain.

THOMAS AQUINAS

In medieval theology, another dominant figure is Thomas Aquinas. He too was born to a wealthy family, the son of the Count of Aquina, in 1225. However, Aquinas shocked his family by becoming a Dominican monk at the age of nineteen. He wrote widely, from commentaries on Scripture to philosophical works. In his discussion of the cross, Aquinas stressed the seriousness of sin: 'A sinful act makes a person punishable in that he violates the order of divine justice.'[16] Unless punishment to meet the demands of divine justice takes place, sin cannot be taken away. But in the death of Christ sin is dealt with in a way that reveals both the love and justice of God:

---

14 **Bernard of Clairvaux,** The Errors of Peter Abelard, 6, 16–7,17, quoted in A. Lane, Lion Concise Book of Christian Thought (Tring: Lion, 1984). p. 87.

15 **Bernard,** Errors of Abelard, quoted in **A.A. Hodge,** Atonement, p. 265.

16 **T. Aquinas,** Summa Theologiae, 1a 2ae 87, 6 (London: Eyre and Spottiswood, 1981).

With justice, because by his passion Christ made satisfaction for the sin of the human race, and man was freed through the justice of Christ. With mercy, because, since man was by himself unable to satisfy for the sin of all human nature ... God gave him his Son to do so.[17]

The idea of satisfaction used by Aquinas is not simply one of God's honour being satisfied, but of 'superabundant atonement for the sins of mankind.' This work of atonement deals not only with sin, but also the just wrath of God against sin.[18] The debt of punishment for sin owed to God has therefore been paid:

By sin man was held to the debt of divine punishment according to the debt of divine justice ... Christ's passion provided adequate and more than adequate satisfaction for man's sin and debt. His passion was, as it were, the price of punishment by which we are freed from both obligations.[19]

The atoning death of Christ is therefore rooted in the love of God, and reveals both his mercy and justice.

Aquinas added to this teaching ideas that Protestants would later take issue with. However, at the heart of his understanding of the cross was that Christ's death was substitutionary, that it dealt with sin and the debt of punishment that was owing, and so satisfied the justice of God. The work of the cross redeems sinners from slavery and punishment. That this view was maintained by such an important thinker in later medieval Catholicism, as it had been in the early church period, is most significant.

Certainly there have been times when different aspects of biblical teaching on the work of Christ have been emphasised, often helpfully so. Medieval theologians took a variety of approaches to the atonement, and left a somewhat mixed legacy. Nonetheless, the view that on the cross Christ was bearing the punishment for sin, and was doing this in a

---

17 Aquinas, *Summa*, 3a. 46. 2.
18 Aquinas, *Summa*, 3a. 48. 2; 3a 49. 4.
19 Aquinas, *Summa*, 3, 48, 4; 3, 54, 85.

substitutionary way, was maintained not only during the early period of the church, but also by leading medieval theologians such as Gregory, John of Damascus, Bernard of Clairvaux and Thomas Aquinas, and has lain at the heart of Christian orthodoxy. Abelard found that to veer far from this line was to be subject to strong opposition—and even he found it hard to avoid using the language of substitution.

JOHN WYCLIFFE

In the following centuries, what was accomplished through the death of Christ was to be taught with renewed clarity. One of the forerunners of the Reformation, its 'Morning Star,' was John Wycliffe (c.1329–1384), and his views underline the continuity of Christian teaching on the subject. To him the key was the justice of God. It would not have been just for God simply to forgive sin:

It is a light word to say that God might, of his power, forgive this sin [Adam's] without the aseeth [satisfaction] which was made for it … but his justice would not suffer it, but requires that each trespass be punished either on earth or in hell. And God may not accept a person to forgive him without satisfaction.[20]

Only the substitutionary death of the Son of God meets the just demands of God—the penalty for sin has been paid. In Christ 'trespass' has been punished, and justice satisfied. The way to forgiveness is now open for the believer. The full understanding of this amazing truth was to transform lives in the following centuries.

---

20 J. **Wycliffe,** *De Incarnatione et Morte Christi,* in **A.A. Hodge,** *Atonement,* p. 265.

The atonement in the Reformation and Puritan Era

'This Doctrine So Sweet and So Filled With Comfort'[1]

What the Reformers had to say about the atonement was not original. However, with their close attention to the biblical text and their conviction of its final authority, together with their understanding of salvation by God's grace alone through faith, they were able to express what had been written before with renewed clarity. In the Reformation the discussion of the atonement itself did not play a central place in theological controversy between Protestant and Catholic scholars. Whilst they differed on the way that the fruits of the atonement were applied to the believer, both Protestant and Catholic thinkers agreed that the death of Christ was a work of propitiation.

MARTIN LUTHER

For years Martin Luther (1483–1546) agonised under the burden of his sense of sinfulness. When he became a monk in 1505 he wrestled long and hard with the conviction that he was not worthy to stand in God's presence. He drove himself to the limits of his human strength as he tried everything the medieval Roman Catholic Church had to offer in an unsuccessful attempt to gain relief from this sense of guilt and condemnation. At the heart of his struggle was a quest for assurance. Help was to eventually come through the teaching of the Bible, coupled with the wise advice of his confessor to look for help in 'the wounds of the most sweet Saviour.'[2]

---

1 **M. Luther,** *Luther's Works: Lectures on Galatians Chapters 1–4, 1535,* **eds. J. Pelikan and W.A. Hansen** (St Louis: Concordia, 1963), p. 280.

2 **Luther,** *Works of Martin Luther.* Vol 48, **ed J. Pelikan and W.A. Hansen** (St Louis: Concordia and Philadelphia: Fortress Press, 1958–1986), p. 66.

After he became Doctor of Theology in 1512, and was appointed Lecturer in Biblical Theology at Wittenberg University, the answer to his spiritual need gradually unfolded as he taught his way through different books of the Bible. His lectures on Romans were of particular importance. Luther had no doubt as to the reality of sin, his own experience proved that; nor did he doubt the wrath of God, as shown in his comments on Romans 2:8: 'I take this to mean the wrath of indignation or wrath of anger which God sends upon body and soul; it is the wrath of his severity.' Because God is holy and just, sin must be punished: God's 'wrath abides upon [sin] eternally and irrevocably.'[3]

Luther's great emphasis was that human merit has no place in the way of salvation. Sin has spoiled every aspect of humanity, even good deeds and religious acts. Salvation is accomplished only through the work of Christ upon the cross. Luther argued that Romans 3:25, a 'perplexing and difficult text', demonstrates how:

God from eternity has ordained and set forth Christ as the propitiation for our sins, but that only for those who believe in Him. Christ wanted to become a propitiation for us only through His blood, that is, He first had to make amends for us through the shedding of His blood.

Being put right with God therefore, rests exclusively on the saving work of Christ at Calvary, we 'must obtain our righteousness solely from God, now that forgiveness for our sins has been secured by Christ's atonement.'[4]

Luther lectured on Galatians in 1516–17, and revised his work in 1535. His discussion of Galatians 3:13 is a detailed consideration of the atonement, which he called 'the adorable mysteries of scripture.' He pondered deeply, as the early church Fathers had done, the way in which Christ redeemed the believer from the curse of the law, by being made a curse for us. Christ was 'innocent as concerning his own person', so his death was not for his deeds. To Luther, the words 'for us' in Galatians 3:13 were crucial:

---

3 **Martin Luther,** *Lectures on Romans,* **trans. and ed. by W. Pauck** (Philadelphia: Westminster Press, 1961), pp. 44–45.

4 **M. Luther,** *Lectures on Romans,* Romans 3:25 (Michigan: Kregel, 1976), p. 78.

We are sinners and thieves, and therefore are worthy of death and eternal damnation. But Christ took all our sins upon Himself, and for them He died on the cross.

The incarnation and the cross are inextricably linked—'But just as Christ is wrapped up in our flesh and blood, so we must wrap Him, and know Him to be wrapped up in our sins, our curse, our death, and everything evil.'[5] To Luther, the work of Christ as sin-bearer was so absolute that upon the cross he actually became 'the greatest thief, murderer, adulterer, robber, desecrator, blasphemer, etc, there has ever been any where in the world.' Christ carried the sin of Paul, 'the persecutor, blasphemer, and assaulter', of David 'the adulterer', and so on, 'that he might pay and make satisfaction for them.'[6] Although some feel Luther went too far in what he states here, the point is clear: the sinless Christ is numbered among the transgressors and bears their sin, and the consequences of that sin: 'For all the curses of the Law were gathered together in Him, and therefore He bore and sustained them in his own body for us. Consequently, He was not only accursed, but He became a curse for us.'[7]

Luther drew Isaiah 53:5–6 into his discussion, especially the phrase: 'The Lord has laid on him the iniquity of us all.' He stressed, 'These words must not be diluted but must be left in their precise and serious sense.' If Christ is truly to be the bearer of sin, and the guilt associated with that sin, then he must bear the punishment for sinners. Sin bearing and punishment cannot be separated, as he stresses repeatedly: 'Why is Christ punished? Is it not because He has and bears sin?'[8] Luther summed up 'this doctrine, so sweet and full of comfort', concisely:

When the merciful Father saw that we were being oppressed through the Law, he ... sent His Son into the world, and heaped all the sins of men upon Him, and said to Him ... be

---

5 Martin Luther, *Luther's Works: Lectures on Galatians Chapters 1–4* (1535), pp. 290, 277–78.

6 Luther, *Galatians,* p. 280.

7 Luther, *Galatians,* p. 289.

8 Luther, *Galatians,* pp. 278–79.

the person … who has committed the sins of all men. And see to it that you pay and make satisfaction for them.

The death of Jesus Christ therefore satisfies the demands of justice, the debt is paid, the 'believer is delivered.' If this is not so, then 'we carry them and shall die and be damned in them,'[9] but we can be assured that Christ has 'put himself in opposition to sin, death, the curse of the law, and the wrath and judgement of God, and overcome them in his body.' The cost of this to Christ was immense: 'It is something awful to bear sin, the wrath of God, the curse and death.'[10] Whereas Anselm had argued that the choice for God was punishment or satisfaction. Luther argued that God chooses both: in the death of Christ the punishment for sin is borne, and because punishment is paid, justice is satisfied.

Luther made it clear that the death of Christ is an act of penal substitution: all our evils 'which were supposed to oppress and torment us eternally, overwhelmed him once, for a brief time.' He does not hesitate to speak of the wrath of God when speaking of the cross, applying Psalm 88:7 and 16 to the cross: 'Thy wrath lies heavy upon Me and Thou dost overwhelm me with all Thy waves' and 'Thy wrath has swept over me.' The fruits of this substitutionary death are immense—'Being delivered in this way from these eternal terrors and torments by Christ, we shall enjoy eternal and indescribable peace and joy provided that we believe this.'[11] It takes one 'of such precious worth' to atone for sin, 'assume its guilt, pay the price of the wrath and thus abolish sin.' Indeed, only God's Son could 'take upon himself the load of awful and eternal wrath and make his own body and blood a sacrifice for sin. And he did so, out of the immeasurable great mercy and love towards us, giving himself up and bearing the sentence of unending wrath and death.'[12]

---

9 **Luther,** *Galatians,* p. 280.

10 **Luther,** *Galatians,* pp. 287–88.

11 **Luther,** *Galatians,* p. 290.

12 **M. Luther,** *Epistle Sermon, Twenty-fourth Sunday after Trinity,* **ed. J.N. Lenker** (Minneapolis: Luther Press), 60: 9, 43, in McDonald, *Atonement,* p. 182.

The cross was, to Luther, the supreme act of a loving God: 'Therefore Christ was not only crucified and died, but by divine love sin was laid upon him.'[13] It was an act freely done: 'Christ himself voluntarily became a curse for us', as Luther stressed—'Because He took upon Himself our sins, not by compulsion but of His own free will, it was right for Him to bear the punishment and the wrath of God.' Luther also linked the atonement to the resurrection, and the glorious fruits that follow: 'Nor can sin, death, and our mask be found in Him any longer, but there is sheer righteousness, life, and eternal blessing.'[14]

In his work, the 'Freedom of a Christian' Luther summarised the way of salvation by using the picture of a marriage. Faith, he argued,

Unites the soul with Christ as a bride is united with her bridegroom ... By the wedding ring of faith he shares in the sins, death, and hell which are his bride's. As a matter of fact, he makes them his own and acts as if they were his own and as if he himself had sinned; he suffered, died and descended into hell that he might overcome them all ... Here this rich and divine bridegroom Christ, marries this poor, wicked harlot, redeems her from all evil, and adorns her with all his goodness. Her sins cannot now destroy her, since they are laid upon Christ, and swallowed up by him. And she has that righteousness in Christ, her husband, of which she may boast as of her own ...[15]

Luther noted how often the doctrine of the cross was under attack from 'the devil and the sectarians' who, 'with their perverse and wicked doctrine are bent on this one thing: to obscure this doctrine and take it away from us.' However, he was determined to insist on it: 'so diligently that we bear the hate and persecution of Satan and the world. For Satan feels the power and results of this doctrine.'[16]

This gospel met Luther in his need when he was first converted. He continued to believe that 'this is the most joyous of all doctrines and one

---

13 **Luther,** *Galatians,* p. 279.

14 **Luther,** *Galatians,* p. 284.

15 **Luther,** *Works,* Vol. 31. pp. 351–52.

16 **Luther,** *Galatians,* p. 285.

that entertains the most comfort.' As a pastor as well as a theologian, Luther realised that here was help for those struggling with sin and guilt.[17] Against those who argued that the substitutionary death of Christ was not a motivation to good works, Luther had a strong response: 'Once we have been justified by faith we enter the active life … [which] exercises itself in works of love toward one's neighbour.'[18] The cross was, to Luther, that against which all theological statements should be judged and understood. In the weakness and brokenness of the cross, God's power is supremely revealed; his love is most truly displayed in Christ's willing submission to the full weight of sin, guilt and wrath upon the cross. Suffering can only make sense when viewed through the cross, as Luther declared in 1518: 'He deserves to be called a theologian, however, who comprehends the visible and manifest things of God seen through suffering and the cross.'[19]

Luther certainly used other ways of talking about the cross—such as that of victory, or overcoming: 'Christ the divine power, Righteousness, Blessing, Grace, and Life, conquers and destroys these monsters—sin, death, and the curse, without weapons or battle, in His own body, and in himself.' But this work of victory is only possible if Christ's work is one of propitiation: 'If you look at this Person Christ, therefore, you see sin, death, the wrath of God, hell, the devil, and all evils conquered and put to death in him.' Luther was in no doubt that the victorious, atoning death of Christ is the 'chief doctrine of the Christian faith.' It holds together and explains other central Christian doctrines.[20] Upon it rested the central doctrines of justification by faith, so vital to his spiritual 'breakthrough', and of the incarnation: 'When we teach that men are justified by Christ, and that Christ is the victor over sin, death, and the eternal curse, we are testifying at the same time that He is God by nature.'[21]

---

17 **Luther,** *Galatians,* p. 280.

18 **Luther,** *Galatians,* p. 287.

19 **M. Luther,** 'Heidelberg Disputation: 40 Theses for Debate', Thesis 20, in **T.F. Lull. (ed.),** *Martin Luther's Basic Theological Writings* (Minneapolis: Fortress Press, 1989), p. 31.

20 **Luther,** *Galatians,* p. 282.

21 **Luther,** *Galatians,* p. 283.

The implication is clear: If the work of Christ was not to bear the sin of sinners and the punishment of a holy God against that sin, so making justification possible, why was the incarnation necessary? If the death of Christ is something less than an act of propitiation, God reconciling sinners to God by bearing the eternal punishment for sin, one who was less than God could have sufficed. To attack the doctrine of the atonement is in fact to attack the incarnation.

JOHN CALVIN

Luther's conviction that the atonement lay at the heart of theology was shared by the great reformer of Geneva, John Calvin (1509–64). Although he revealed less of his personal spiritual struggles, Calvin remained at heart a practical theologian; his ideas were worked out in his regular preaching and pastoral ministry. As with Luther, he stressed the importance of recognising the enormity of the problem of sin in gaining a proper understanding of the atonement. Calvin observed in his commentary on Isaiah 53: 'If we do not perceive our wretchedness and poverty, we shall never know how desirable is that remedy which Christ has brought to us, or approach him with due ardour of affection'.[22] The effect of sin is tragic, it leaves us sighing and groaning for 'that lost worthiness'. It is 'a hereditary depravity and corruption of our nature, diffused into all parts of the soul, which first makes us liable to God's wrath, then also brings forth in us those works which Scripture calls "works of the flesh".'[23]

The ugliness of sin makes the glory of what God has done in Christ shine all the brighter. The cross is the place of God's supreme demonstration of his love for the sinner, but also of his anger against sin. If he had not loved us he would have made no effort at our reconciliation. Calvin shows in his comments on Romans 5:8–10 that there is no disconnection between the wrath of God and the love of God: 'In a marvellous and divine way he loved us even when he hated us. For he hated us for what we were that he had not

---

22 **J. Calvin,** *Commentary on the Book of the Prophet Isaiah, Vol. 4.* (Grand Rapids: Eerdmans, 1956). Comments on Isaiah 53:6. p. 117.

23 **J. Calvin,** *Institutes of the Christian Religion,* **ed. J.T. McNeill** (Philadelphia: Westminster, 1960), Book II, 1, iii, and viii. pp. 244, 251.

made; yet because our wickedness had not entirely consumed his handiwork, he knew how, at the same time, to hate in each one of us what we had made, and to love what he had made.'[24]

Calvin described the atonement in terms of penal substitution. First, it deals with the problem of sin, and the just anger of God against it:

God's righteous curse bars our access to him, and God in his capacity as judge is angry toward us. Hence, an expiation must intervene in order that Christ as priest may obtain God's favour for us and appease his wrath.

In dealing with sin, God's wrath against it was turned away by Christ,[25] who in death

was offered to the Father as a propitiatory victim; that, expiation being made by his sacrifice, we might cease to tremble at the divine wrath.

Calvin defined a sacrifice of 'expiation' as one 'upon which our stain and punishment might somehow be cast, and cease to be imputed to us.' As such a sacrifice, Christ 'interposed', and 'took upon himself and suffered the punishment that, from God's righteous judgement, threatened all sinners.'[26]

Through the course of these awesome events, the love of the Father for the Son never ceased: 'How could he be angry toward his beloved Son, "in whom his heart reposed"?' While 'utterly clean of all fault', on the cross he nonetheless took on himself 'the shame and reproach of our iniquities', so that when he 'discharged all satisfaction through his sacrifice, we might cease to be afraid of God's wrath.' It becomes clear that 'he suffers for another's and not for his own crime.' We must not diminish the cost of what the Son of God endured, as he underwent 'the severity of God's vengeance, to appease his wrath, and satisfy his just judgement.'

Christ's work was a clear act of substitution: 'Christ was put in place of evildoers as surety and pledge ... to bear and suffer all the punishments that

24 Calvin, *Institutes*, II, 16, 4. pp. 506–07.

25 Calvin, *Institutes*, II, 15, 6. pp. 501–02.

26 Calvin, *Institutes*, II, 16, 6. pp. 510–11; II, 16, 2, p. 505.

they ought to have sustained.' His substitutionary suffering cannot simply be confined to the physical realm, but we should never forget the 'invisible and incomprehensible judgement which he underwent in the sight of God ... he paid a greater and more excellent price in suffering in his soul the terrible torments of a condemned and forsaken man.'[27]

The richness of biblical material about the cross is reflected in Calvin's thinking. He uses the image of victory, as he declares: 'In taking the curse upon himself, he crushed, broke, and scattered its whole force ... Paul with good reason, therefore, magnificently proclaims the triumph Christ obtained for himself on the cross, as if the cross, which was full of shame, had been changed into a triumphal chariot.' Nor does he confine the work of atonement to the hours at Calvary, but draws the whole life of Christ into the picture: 'From the time when he took on the form of a servant, he began to pay the price of liberation in order to redeem us.'[28] Therefore Christ's saving work involves his active obedience in life, and supremely his passive obedience in death—the two are closely linked together. The work of Christ after Calvary was not ignored either; even after the ascension, his work continued: 'By his intercession he propitiates God to us and sanctifies our prayers by the odour of his sacrifice.'[29]

At the heart of these rich ways of speaking of the cross is a clear and compelling statement of the reason for the atonement. Sin demands punishment, the moral law cannot be infringed, so in the loving way of salvation that God offers through the cross, justice is done, but mercy is shown. In salvation God must be true to his own character: 'We cannot get grace without justice ... can God deny himself? Can he divest himself of his holiness, justice and integrity?'[30] The mechanism by which the love and justice of God are to be held together in the cross did not trouble Calvin,

---

27 Calvin, *Institutes,* II, 16, 11, p. 517; II, 16, 6. p. 510; II, 16, 10, pp. 515–16.

28 Calvin, *Institutes,* II, 16, 6, p. 511; II, 16, 5, p. 507.

29 J. Calvin, Commentary on 1 John 2:1 in *Calvin's New Testament Commentaries,* Vol. 5 (Grand Rapids: Eerdmans, 1959), p. 244.

30 Calvin, 'Sixth Sermon on the Passion', *Calvin's Works,* 56:910, quoted by **H. Blocher** in 'The Atonement in John Calvin's Theology', in *The Glory of the Atonement* (**ed. C.E. Hill**) (Downer's Grove, Illinois: IVP, 2004), p. 299.

instead as J.I. Packer puts it: 'His only interest is in the mysterious but blessed fact that at the cross God did act in both love and justice to save us from our sins.'[31] Nonetheless, it should never be argued that Calvin simply had a harsh and mechanical view of the atonement—to him the suffering of Christ was a 'testimony of the incomparable love he had for us.'[32]

The view of Luther, that the penal substitutionary understanding of the cross is highly relevant to living the Christian life, was shared by Calvin. The death of Christ does not need to be turned into a mere moral example to produce fruits in the life of the believer. Indeed these fruits should be manifest in the believer, unless: 'They intend to render his death useless and unfruitful.' The death of Christ becomes the source of all spiritual blessing, as Calvin summed up his discussion of the atonement: 'since rich store of every kind of good abounds in him, let us drink our fill from this fountain, and from no other.'[33]

ZWINGLI AND BUCER

Luther and Calvin are the most well-known of the reformers, but their view of the atonement was shared by many others. In Zurich, Ulrich Zwingli (1484–1531) was a leading figure in the Reformation in Switzerland. A contemporary of Luther, he held similar views to his German counterpart. He affirmed that Christ offered a substitutionary death for the sin of God's people:

Christ was without sin, and guile was not found in his mouth … And yet he died this death, he suffered in our stead. He was willing to die, that he might restore us to life; and as he had no sins of his own, the all-merciful Father laid ours upon him.[34]

Another significant Reformer was Martin Bucer (1491–1551), who took a key role in the work of reformation at Strasbourg. John Calvin worked with him

---

31 J.I. Packer, 'What Did the Cross Achieve?', *Tyndale Bulletin* 25 (1974), p. 5.

32 Calvin, *Institutes* II, 16, 5, p. 508.

33 Calvin, *Institutes*, II, 16, 7, p. 512; II, 16, 1, p. 528.

34 U. Zwingli, *Works*. I, p. 204, quoted in **A.A. Hodge,** *Nature of the* Atonement, p. 267.

for three important years from 1538–41, learning much from the pattern of church practice he had established. Bucer's pastoral instructions for the 'Visitation of the Sick' contain words for those troubled by guilt and seeking forgiveness from God. The seriousness of sin was stressed: 'We have offended against God and sundered ourselves from him who is life and gives life, and been plunged in eternal death.' It is impossible to return to spiritual life with God unless it is through the 'death and the offering of [Christ's] body and blood', for he is the substitute for sinners, the one 'on whom the Father has laid all our transgressions and whom for our sake he has smitten and delivered up for our sins.' For those in spiritual need, this way, and this alone, brings 'satisfaction for our sins and eternal reconciliation with God the Father.'[35]

ANGLICAN AND ANABAPTIST VIEWS

At the heart of the Anglican communion service since 1549 has been the affirmation by Thomas Cranmer (1489–1556) of the substitutionary work of Christ as, 'a full, perfect, and sufficient sacrifice, oblation, and satisfaction for the sins of the whole world.'[36] In his *Defence of the True Doctrine of the Sacraments* Cranmer explained his understanding of how the cross was a 'sufficient sacrifice':

One kind of sacrifice there is which is called a propitiatory or merciful sacrifice; that is to say, such a sacrifice as pacifies God's wrath and indignation, and obtains mercy and forgiveness for all our sins, and it is the ransom for the redemption from everlasting damnation. There is but one such sacrifice, whereby our sins are pardoned and God's mercy and favour obtained; which is the death of the Son of God, our Lord Jesus Christ.[37]

---

35 M. Bucer, 'Visitation of the Sick', *Common Places of Martin Bucer,* **ed. D.F. Wright** (Appleford: Sutton Courtney Press, 1972), pp. 444–445.

36 'Order for the Administration of the Lord's Supper, or Holy Communion', *Book of Common Prayer (1559)* in **D. Cressy and L.A. Ferrell,** *Religion and Society in Early Modern England: A Sourcebook* (London: Routledge, 1996), p. 47. The same wordage is found in the 1549 and 1552 editions of the Prayer Book, but the spelling is more antiquated.

37 T. Cranmer, *Defence of the True Doctrine of the* Sacraments, Book V, 3. quoted in **Hodge,** *Nature of the Atonement,* p. 268.

Michael Sattler was a leading figure amongst the Evangelical Anabaptists, a group of reformers who rejected a connection between church and state and, along with that, the practice of infant baptism. They stressed the importance of the plain sense of Scripture. In his work: *On the Satisfaction of Christ,* Sattler, a former monk who was later to die a heroic martyr's death for his faith, summarised what Scripture says of the atonement in his paraphrase of Romans 3:25

[We] are all together sinners and fall short of the praise which God should have from [us], and are justified without merit, by his grace, through the redemption worked by Christ, whom God sent forth as a mercy seat, through faith in his blood, so that he might demonstrate the righteousness which is valid before, under divine patience, which suffered, etc.

The image of the 'mercy seat', the place of atonement prefigured in the Old Testament sacrificial system and fulfilled with the death of Christ upon the cross, was repeatedly used by Sattler. So too was the idea of penal substitution. Quoting Isaiah 53, 'We are healed by his stripes', Sattler affirms with other Scripture references that by this means, the righteous demands of a holy God are met, Christ is 'the justice and wisdom of the believers [1 Corinthians 1]', and alone is 'our reconciliation [1 John 2].'[38]

SOCINUS' CHALLENGE TO TRADITIONAL TEACHING

The understanding of the death of Christ as being a work of propitiation was not an area of significant theological conflict between Protestants and Catholics at the time of the Reformation. Even the Council of Trent, which sat from 1545 to 1563, and restated Roman Catholic doctrine in the light of the Protestant Reformation, argued that, 'The first and most excellent satisfaction is that by which whatever is due by us to God, on account of our sins, has been paid abundantly ... according to the strict rigour of his justice'. This satisfaction of Christ has rendered God 'propitious' to us,

---

38 **M. Sattler,** 'On the Satisfaction of Christ', in *The Legacy of Michael Sattler,* (**trans. J.H. Yoder**) (Pennsylvania: Herald Press, Scottdale, 1973), ch VII, pp. 108–114. Yoder notes that the word translated 'satisfaction' can also be translated 'atonement'.

and we are 'indebted to Christ the Lord alone, who having paid the price of our sins on the cross, most fully satisfied God.'[39] The major debates between Protestant and Catholic theologians instead focussed upon the way the fruits of the infinite satisfaction of the justice of God, accomplished on the cross were applied to the believer. This made justification by grace through faith an area of disagreement, along with the nature of the church and its sacraments, and the authority of Scripture.

Significant challenges to traditional ways of thinking about the atonement came through the work of extreme radicals, who, in the climate of more open theological thought in the Reformation, began to question a wide range of orthodox teaching. One such was Faustus Socinus, an Italian, who lived for a short period in Basle, before moving to work in Cracow, Poland, in the later part of the sixteenth century. To Socinus, God was a sovereign king, rather than a sovereign judge, who could simply decide from his own sovereign will to forgive sins. He did not believe that upon the cross Christ bore either sin or the punishment for it. The fundamental problem Socinus had was with the concept of God's 'justice' —'If we could but get rid of this justice, even if we have no other proof, this fiction of Christ's satisfaction would be thoroughly exposed, and should vanish.' To him punishment and forgiveness were incompatible: sin should either be punished or forgiven, not both. Socinus also questioned the idea of a substitution of one for another guilty person: it might be possible to pay debts for another, but sin is a personal matter, and cannot be laid to another's account. Therefore in salvation, Socinus argued, God set aside his justice, and acted simply in a display of mercy.[40]

One crucial aspect of the character of God was rejected by Socinus—his absolute and constant justice. The teaching of Scripture on this, and God's righteousness and holiness, is little considered. He replaced the sovereign

---

39 'Catechism of the Council of Trent', Part II, Ch. 5, question 60, quoted in **A.A. Hodge,** *Outlines of Theology* (1879) (reprinted Edinburgh: Banner of Truth, 1983), p. 424. When used by Catholic theologians at the Council of Trent the term 'satisfaction' could be read more in terms of Anselm's teaching, rather than with the meaning invested in it by the Reformers.

40 F. Socinus, *De Jesu Christo Servatore*, 3, 1, in McDonald, p. 197.

Judge, with a more arbitrary Ruler, who has the absolute right to forgive—
if he chooses to do so. The problem Socinus had with the idea of
transference of guilt shows how heavily he was constrained by the concepts
of human logic and law; he fails to see that with God things are possible
that are not possible to us. Socinus was also left struggling to explain the
horror of the cross: 'Why should God have willed to kill his innocent Son by
a cruel and execrable death when there was no need of satisfaction?'
Instead of seeing the death of Christ as the means by which he reconciles
the sinner to a holy God, the cross is reduced to a spectacle principally
designed to inspire us 'to accept the pardon offered and to put our faith in
Christ himself.'[41] It is intended to shock sinners into a response of
obedience and faith.

Socinus's move away from the traditional understanding of the cross
was inseparable from his unorthodox beliefs in other areas. He took a
very rationalistic approach to Scripture. Although he accepted that
Christ was the revelation of God, he believed he was merely a man,
supreme teacher, announcer and example of the way of salvation, but
not God the Son. Socinus largely repeats Abelard's teaching that Christ
is the supreme moral influence, a mighty teacher. He ends up with a
Christ who is not God, who did not make atonement for humans who are
not truly sinners. Elements of what Socinus taught, though rejected by
the mainstream of the church at the time, were to prove very influential
upon later thinkers. As Athanasius and the church Councils of Nicea
and Chalcedon showed early in the church: a correct understanding of
the cross is inseparable from a correct understanding of the deity of
Christ.

THE RESPONSE OF GROTIUS

A robust challenge to Socinus came from the Dutch thinker Hugo Grotius
(1583–1645). He believed that Socinus' questioning of the orthodox
catholic doctrine of the atonement, was a challenge to that which had
been agreed upon by Christians in all ages. Grotius argued that God was

---

41 Socinus, *De Jesu Christo,* 1, 4.

The atonement in the Reformation and Puritan era

moved by his goodness to bring benefit to humanity, but was hindered by the problem of sin which deserved punishment. For God to exercise mercy, his justice must in some way be satisfied; God cannot simply forgive, as Socinus had argued. Instead, Grotius explained, God determined that 'Christ voluntarily out of his love towards men should pay the penalty of our sins by enduring the sorest torments and shameful death, that we, subject to the demonstrations of God's justice, should, on condition of true faith, be freed from the penalty of eternal death.'[42] Grotius stresses that the death of Christ was an act of penal substitution, in which he bore the punishment due to sin: 'Here [in Isaiah 53:11] it is said expressly that Christ will bear the punishment of those who are made righteous ... To bear sins by suffering, and in such a way as to liberate others, can only mean to take upon oneself another's punishment.'[43] He also argued although this is of secondary importance in the atonement, that this is an act of deterrence by the sovereign Ruler of the universe, a 'penal example', for the good of the community. The cross was a public demonstration of the justice of God's rule, affirming that the world has a just Ruler.

One question that Grotius wrestled with was how such a sovereign Ruler and Judge could let the punishment of one innocent person, in this case Christ, discharge the guilt of other sinful persons, who then go free. He argued that God granted a relaxation, or dispensation, of the law, which allowed the sentence due to sinners to be applied to Christ. This has led to the widely held view that Grotius taught that Christ only met the relaxed demands of the law, the substitute for a penalty, rather than the exact equivalent of the punishment of sin. Recent scholarship has significantly challenged this view. Although Grotius taught that the punishment Christ bore for sinners is different from that which the sinners themselves would have had to bear, the difference is primarily that it was borne by a substitute who was not a sinner, and not personally accountable for the sins he was

---

42 **H. Grotius,** *Defensio Fidei Catholice de Satisfactione Christi* (1636), quoted in McDonald, p. 203.

43 **Grotius,** *De Satisfactione Christi,* I, 24, 102–103; I. 26, 104–05.

The Divine Substitute **91**

bearing. To Grotius, therefore, in the death of Christ a full and real punishment for sin is paid, and a penal example is also offered, demonstrating that sin brings a punishment.[44]

THE PURITANS

The Puritan movement was an attempt to apply at local community level the fruits of the English Reformation. The work of the Puritans was Bible-centred, with a strong emphasis on preaching, and it was also cross-centred.

RICHARD SIBBES

In his 1634 sermon 'Christ's sufferings for man's sin', the Puritan, Richard Sibbes, took his congregation to the cry of dereliction in Matthew 27:46, and profoundly explored the issue of what was being accomplished upon the cross. Sibbes held positions of great influence within Cambridge University, but was also a fine pastor known for his gentle, personal godliness. It was said of Sibbes 'heaven was in him before he was in heaven.' Yet, whilst deeply concerned for broken and struggling Christians, and constantly emphasising the love of God, he does not feel the need to spare his hearers from an understanding of the cross in terms of penal substitution. Instead, the pastoral desire to bring peace and assurance to troubled sinners motivates him to explore the horror and the triumph of the cross.

Sibbes demonstrated that the utter ugliness of sin was something that God could not endure, and it left debts of both obedience and punishment. However, Christ willingly came to deal with the problem of disobedience, by his own perfect obedience, and then with the need for sin to be punished, by dying upon the cross to pay the penalty for sin. Christ willingly endured the full punishment due for sin—the judgement of God against it, as the cry

---

44 We are grateful to Dr Garry Williams for his comments on this chapter. His D. Phil. thesis, 'A Critical Exposition of Hugo Grotius's Doctrine of the Atonement in *De satisfactione Christi*', (Oxford: University of Oxford Press, 1999), significantly challenges the common view that Grotius is the author of the 'governmental theory' of the atonement in which Christ bears a relaxed version of the law, and only a substitute for the full penalty of sin.

of dereliction shows. As Sibbes concluded his sermon, the pastoral application lessons poured out: because we have a divine peacemaker, we can 'go boldly to the throne of grace through him'; when troubled by sin and fear of hell, we can plead that God's justice is satisfied in what Christ has done. Those struggling with darkness and difficulty can see that Christ 'struggled with the powers of darkness and the wrath of his Father a while, but presently, after, all was finished'; and the believer can know that there is a crown of righteousness stored up. As he closed, 'What a stay is this for a distressed soul to make use of!' How different from those who today argue that struggling Christians should be spared from such teaching![45]

JOHN OWEN

Many ordinary Puritan parish ministers were significant theologians in their own right, but John Owen stands pre-eminent amongst Puritan thinkers. He began parish ministry in Essex in 1643, but after working as a chaplain in the Civil War, he was appointed Dean of Christ Church, Oxford, in 1651, and a year later became vice-chancellor of Oxford University. Although removed from his position on the restoration of the Monarchy in 1660, he continued to write a great range of significant works of theology, including a commentary on Hebrews, and an exposition of the atonement—*The Death of Death in the Death of Christ*. In this work Owen demonstrated how the death of Christ is the fitting way of salvation for believers. The death of Christ is an exact equivalent for the sins of all Christian believers, the punishment he bears is the same as that which they should have borne: 'When I say *the same*, I mean essentially the same in weight and pressure, though not in all accidents of duration and the like; for it was impossible he should be detained by death.'

Owen showed how the death of Christ satisfies the demands of justice, and frees believers from the wrath of God they deserved. He was made a curse, that they might be spared from the curse; he was made sin to deliver believers from sin; he underwent death to deliver believers from death:

---

45 R. Sibbes, 'Christ's Suffering for Man's Sin' (1634), in *Works of Richard Sibbes*, Vol I., ed. A.B. Grosart (reprinted Edinburgh: Banner of Truth, 1979).

Neither do we read of any relaxation of the punishment in the Scriptures, but only a commution [exchange] of the person; which being done 'God condemned sin in the flesh of his Son'.[46]

Owen stressed that because of the union of believers with Christ, on the cross he stands 'in their room and stead.' Christ, 'federal head' over the one body the Church, is the penal substitute: 'the surety is the head, those represented by him the members; and when the head is punished, the members also are punished.'[47]

STEPHEN CHARNOCK

In his magisterial work *The Existence and Attributes of God*, based upon what he preached to his congregation, another Puritan, Stephen Charnock, discussed the sovereignty of God, and how this affects the transference of our sins to Christ. The ability to transfer the penalty of the crime from one person to another is dependent upon two things. Firstly, it requires the act of an absolute sovereign to do this. Secondly, it depends upon the consent of the person who willingly consents to suffer in the place of another. On the cross, both these things are demonstrated. Quoting Isaiah 53:6 and 2 Corinthians 5:21 Charnock asserted:

God transferred the sins of men upon Christ, and inflicted on him a punishment for them. He summed up the debt of man, and charged them upon the score of Christ, imputing to him the guilt, and inflicting upon him the penalty.

He stressed that Christ was not an unwilling partner—the action was by 'the consent of Christ and the order of the Judge of the world.' God, who is the 'sole creditor' to whom the debt is owed, accepts the act of the Son in paying the debt: God the Father and God the Son were at one in this. Charnock stressed the full reality of what Christ endured. Bearing the

---

46 **J. Owen,** *The Death of Death in the Death of Christ*, ed. W.H. Goold (London: Banner of Truth, 1959), pp. 157–8, 175, 156–57.

47 **J. Owen,** *Works* (Edinburgh: Banner of Truth, 1967), Vol. 10, p. 598.

wrath of God 'far exceeds the calamity of a mere bodily death'; instead, the wrath of God 'dropped upon his soul, and rendered it so full of agonies.' All this was by imputation, of the sins and punishment to one who was all the while 'holy, harmless, and indefiled.'[48]

JOHN BUNYAN

Bunyan had little schooling or theological education, and worked as a tinker in Bedfordshire. Nonetheless, he became in the Puritan era one of England's greatest preachers. In *The Pilgrim's Progress*, the Pilgrim finds relief from his burden of sin and guilt at the cross, and is able to set out on his journey to the Celestial City. In his writings, Bunyan made frequent mention of the cross, which had proved of great comfort in his own struggle with sin. What he knew from experience, he preached to others: 'The blood of Christ is of infinite value, for he offereth mercy to the biggest of sinners.'[49] Bunyan set out how the death of Christ could be of such 'infinite value.' Christ was the perfect substitute—the sin-bearer 'for the body of Christ was our flesh, upon it also was laid our sin.' In his death Jesus stood 'in our stead', the substitute sent 'on purpose to deliver men from the wrath to come.' All that was the sinner's became Christ's, so that what is Christ's could be the sinner's—the believer is covered by Christ's 'infinite righteousness from the wrath of God.'[50] Bunyan had no doubt that, because of the justice of God, the cross was the only way of salvation—'As there is grace, so there is justice in God ... it was absolutely necessary that Jesus Christ should put himself into our very condition.' Therefore, although 'Man should have been pierced with the spear of God's wrath ... to prevent that, Jesus was pierced by both God and man.'[51]

---

48 S. Charnock, *The Existence and Attributes of God*, Discourse XIII, Vol II, (1682; repr. Edinburgh: R. Carter, 1853), pp. 424–25.

49 J. Bunyan, 'The Jerusalem Sinner Saved' (London, 1691), in *Works of John Bunyan* (Edinburgh: Blackie and Son, 1854), Vol. I, p. 87.

50 Bunyan, 'Justification by an Imputed Righteousness', in *Works of Bunyan*, Vol. I., pp. 304, 333, 328.

51 Bunyan, 'Saved By Grace', in *Works of John Bunyan*, Vol. I, p. 345.

WESTMINSTER CONFESSION OF FAITH

Those who framed the Westminster Confession of Faith in the 1640s (a statement of the theology for the Presbyterian churches) also rooted the need for the cross in the righteous justice of God against sin—'Every sin, both original and actual, being a transgression of the righteous law of God, and contrary thereunto, doth, in its own nature, bring guilt upon the sinner, whereby he is bound over to the wrath of God, and the curse of the law, and so made subject to death, with all miseries, spiritual, temporal, and eternal.'[52] The work of the cross is depicted as truly Trinitarian in nature: although Christ was called to the role of Mediator by 'his Father, who put power and judgement into his hand,' it was freely embraced: 'This office the Lord Jesus did most willingly undertake'; and he offered himself to God 'through the eternal Spirit.' The sufferings of Christ were truly substitutionary, and truly penal. He 'endured most grievous torments immediately in his soul, and most painful sufferings in his body; was crucified, and died; was buried … On the third day he arose from the dead.' The death of Christ dealt with the problem of sin and the justice of God—it 'hath fully satisfied the justice of his Father; and purchased not only reconciliation, but an everlasting inheritance in the kingdom of heaven.'[53] The Westminster Shorter Catechism succinctly summarises the work of Christ as: 'being born … made under the law, undergoing the miseries of this life, the wrath of God, and the cursed death of the cross.'[54]

MATTHEW HENRY

A fitting summary of the teaching of the Reformers and the Puritans is found in Matthew Henry's *Commentary*, compiled in the early eighteenth century:

Never was there such a demonstration of the justice and holiness of God as there was in the death of Christ. It appears that he hates sin, when nothing less than the blood of

---

52 *Westminster Confession of Faith*, VI, vi.

53 *Westminster Confession of Faith*, VI, iv, v.

54 *Westminster Shorter Catechism*, Question 27.

Christ would satisfy for it. Finding sin, though but imputed, upon his own Son, he did not spare him, because he had made himself sin for us, 2 Corinthians 5:21. The iniquities of us all being laid upon him, though he was the Son of his love, yet it pleased the Lord to bruise him, Isaiah 53:10.[55]

---

55 M. Henry, *An Exposition of the Old and New Testament, Vol. VI: Acts to Revelation* (London: James Nisbet, n.d.), On Romans 3:25–26, Point 5.

The atonement in the eighteenth century Evangelical Revival[1]

'Justice Divine is Satisfied'[2]

There is a strong element of continuity between what was taught by the Reformers, and by the leaders of the eighteenth-century Evangelical Revival. From the work of eminent figures such as Jonathan Edwards, George Whitefield and John and Charles Wesley, to unheralded and obscure lay preachers—both Calvinist and Arminian—all preached the gospel urgently, convinced, as John Wesley put it, that nothing in the Christian faith 'is of greater consequence than the doctrine of the Atonement.'[3] Crucial to their understanding of this, was that Christ's saving work on the cross was one of penal substitution.

JONATHAN EDWARDS

Revival touched North America before Britain, and the pre-eminent figure in the New England awakening was Jonathan Edwards (1703–1758). He was, and remains, one of America's greatest theologians, able to combine deep learning in doctrine, with clear and effective communication of the gospel, and deep pastoral concern for his congregations. Edwards saw the redeeming work of Christ as the ultimate reason for the incarnation: 'Christ came into the world on this errand, to offer himself as an

---

1 An earlier version of this chapter appeared in *Foundations*, Autumn 2005.
2 From hymn by **Charles Wesley,** ''Tis finished, the Messias dies,' No 706 in *Wesley's Hymns*, 1876 edition.
3 **J. Wesley,** *Letters of John Wesley* (London: 1931), Vol. 6, p. 297.

atonement, to answer for our desert of punishment.'[4] He drew into his discussion all of Christ's incarnate life: 'All his humiliations, from the first moment of his incarnation to his resurrection, were propitiatory and satisfactory.'[5] Because of the holiness, majesty, and justice of God, sin must be dealt with: 'Justice requires that sin be punished', and because of the dreadfulness of sin: 'with infinite punishment.'

This requirement was met in the death of Christ, where he 'suffered the full punishment of sin that was imputed to him, and offered to God what was fully and completely equivalent to what was owed to the divine justice for our sins.' This is genuine atonement, the full debt to justice was paid, for it 'bears true proportion to the offence.'[6] Yet, for one who infinitely dwelt in the presence of the Father, the cost of this was 'infinitely terrible', as the cry of dereliction (Matthew 27:46) reveals, 'It was an effect of God's wrath that he forsook Christ.'[7]

Edwards showed how preaching about the atonement is vital to evangelism. In a sermon of 1740 he explained the significance of the cross to children, to whom he appears to have been very effective at preaching, with a good number being converted through his ministry; they included four year-old Phoebe Bartlett: 'Christ has died for children. None can conceive what dreadful things Christ has suffered, and all this he suffered not only for grown persons but for children. All children are by nature children of wrath ... But children that live under the gospel have an opportunity to be delivered from hell ... and enjoy rivers of pleasures at God's right-hand forevermore ... They could have had no such opportunity but by it costing Christ his life and undergoing great cruelties and a very tormenting death.'[8]

4 **J. Edwards,** 'The Justice of God in the Damnation of Sinners', *The Works of Jonathan Edwards, Vol. 19, Sermons and Discourses 1734–1738* (New Haven: Yale University Press, 2001), p. 362.

5 **J. Edwards,** 'History of Redemption', Part 2, in *Works of Jonathan Edwards* (London: 1834). Vol. I, p. 574.

6 **Edwards,** 'History of Redemption', pp. 576–77.

7 **J. Edwards,** *Works* (London: Banner of Truth, 1975), Vol. II, p. 575.

8 **J. Edwards,** 'Children Ought to Love the Lord Jesus Christ', in *The Works of Jonathan Edwards, Vol. 22, Sermons and Discourses 1739–42* (New Haven: Yale, 2003), p. 174.

Although renowned for his sermon 'Sinners in the Hand of an Angry God', Edwards set the love of God firmly alongside the justice of God as the reason for the atonement:

How wonderful his love to sinners was, in that he would die for such sin and wickedness, such corruption ... he was willing to undergo great sufferings for that sin and wickedness ... How astonishingly wonderful was this! Where is anything that can parallel this love?

Edwards emphasised the freeness of the sacrifice of Christ: 'It was entirely Christ's own free and voluntary act. Nor was there ever anything done more voluntarily and freely by Christ than offering that sacrifice of his own life.' There was no compulsion in this: 'Compulsion is a thing that is not compatible to the Deity.' Edwards plumbed the profoundest mystery of how suffering and death touched the very heart of the Godhead.[9]

GEORGE WHITEFIELD

Probably the greatest preacher of the Evangelical Revival was George Whitefield (1714–1770). In his powerful proclamations of the gospel he stressed the plight of man owing to sin, and the redemption of Christ, who came 'by his obedience and death to make atonement for man's transgression'.[10] As the Reformers had done, Whitefield repeatedly stressed that justification is by grace alone through faith in Christ; this rested on the work of the cross: 'Nothing but an infinite ransom could satisfy an infinitely offended justice', therefore God sent 'his only and dear Son Jesus Christ (who is God blessed for ever, and who had laid in his bosom from all eternity) to fulfil the covenant of works, and die a cursed, painful and ignominious death for us, and for our salvation.'[11] In a sermon on Abraham's willingness to

---

9 **J. Edwards,** 'The Free and Voluntary Suffering and Death of Christ', *Works of Edwards,* Vol. I, pp. 511, 497.

10 **G. Whitefield,** 'The Seed of the Woman and the Seed of the Serpent', Sermon 1 in *Sermons on Important Subjects by the Rev. George Whitefield* (London: William Tegg, 1854), pp. 42–43.

11 **Whitefield,** 'Of Justification by Christ', Sermon 46 in *Sermons by Whitefield,* p. 525.

offer Isaac on Mount Moriah, Whitefield drew parallels to the work of the cross, which lies at the root of praise and worship:

Think, O believers, think of the love of God, in giving Jesus Christ to be a propitiation for our sins … think how your heavenly Father bound Jesus Christ as his only Son, and offered him upon the altar of his justice, and laid upon him the iniquities of us all.

But then Whitefield added: 'O do not forget to admire infinitely more the dear Lord Jesus, that promised seed, who willingly said, "Lo, I come," though under no obligation to do so, "to do thy will," to obey and die for men.'[12]

JOHN AND CHARLES WESLEY

During the period of the Evangelical Revival and beyond, Methodists who were Arminian in their theology held with equal firmness similar views of the cross. For both John and Charles Wesley, penal substitution was of great importance.[13] On 21 May 1738, after a long spiritual struggle, Charles Wesley (1707–1788) was able to trust in Christ alone for salvation. The blessing that came from this was immense, as he confided in his Journal that day 'I now found myself at peace with God, and rejoiced in hope of loving Christ … I saw that by faith I stood'; as he later wrote in a famous hymn, 'No condemnation now I dread: Jesus, and all in him, is mine!'[14] The conversion of his brother John came a few days later as he listened to Luther's Preface to Romans being read aloud. He felt his 'heart strangely warmed' and was able to trust in Christ alone for salvation, who had taken away his sins and saved him 'from the law of sin and death.'[15] The dawning realisation that through the cross, Jesus Christ had freed them from the condemnation due for their sins, set the hearts of the Wesley

---

12 Whitefield, 'Abraham's Offering Up His Son Isaac', Sermon 3, in *Sermons by Whitefield,* pp. 65–66.

13 C.W. Williams, *John Wesley's Theology Today* (London: Epworth, 1962), p. 83.

14 C. Wesley, *Journal of Charles Wesley,* entry for May 21, 1738, wesley.nnu.edu/charles_wesley/journal; C. Wesley, 'And Can it Be?', Hymn 201 in *Wesley's Hymns* (London: 1876).

15 J. Wesley, *Journal of John Wesley,* Vol. I (London: 1901). p. 97.

brothers aflame, and liberated their ministries. It inevitably became key to their message. Within a year of his conversion Charles Wesley found himself boldly declaring the theme before the University of Oxford:

All the world being wrapped in sin by breaking of the law, God sent his only Son our Saviour Christ into this world to fulfil the law for us, and by the shedding of his most precious blood, to make a sacrifice or amends to his Father for our sins, and assuage his wrath and indignation conceived against us for the same.[16]

The same emphasis echoes through the sermons of John Wesley (1703–1791). This is important, because these were not simply published as a record of what the great leader of Methodism had preached, but they were to be expository models for other preachers, and a summary of Methodist teaching. So, in Sermon V, on Justification by Faith: 'To him that is justified or forgiven ... God will not inflict on that sinner what he deserved to suffer, because the Son of his love hath suffered for him.' The language of propitiation was often used by John Wesley. He wrote in the same sermon: 'Jesus Christ is described as the one, "whom God hath set forth for a propitiation, through faith on his blood", and again as "the whole and sole *propitiation*".' In Sermon CXIX, Wesley summarised the plain tenor of the new covenant, the gospel message as, 'Believe in the Lord Jesus Christ, whom God hath given to be the propitiation for thy sins, and thou shalt be saved.'[17]

In his *Explanatory Notes Upon the New Testament*, the same views are set out with startling clarity. So on Romans 3:25, Wesley wrote:

Whom God set forth—before angels and men, *a propitiation*—To appease an offended God. But if, as some teach, God never was offended, there was no need of this

---

16 C. Wesley, *The Sermons of Charles Wesley*, ed., K.C. Newport (Oxford: Oxford University Press, 2001) Sermon 7, p. 197.

17 J. Wesley, *Sermons on Several Occasions* (London: 1771), Sermon V, 'Justification by Faith', ii, 5; iv, 1; iv, 8. See also Sermon XVII, 'Circumcision of the Heart', i, 7; Sermon LXI, 'The Mystery of Iniquity', ii; Sermon CXXVIII, 'Free Grace', xxix; etc.

propitiation. And if so, Christ died in vain. *To declare his righteousness*—To demonstrate not only his clemency, but his justice ... whose essential character and principal office is, to punish sin.

The atonement demonstrated both God's justice towards sin, which had to be punished, and his mercy, for the just punishment for sin was willingly paid by his Son. It was crucial to Wesley that God should be seen to maintain his justice, as he adds in his comments on the next verse,

The attribute of justice must be preserved inviolate. And inviolate it is preserved, if there was a real infliction of punishment on our Saviour. On this plan all the attributes harmonise. Every attribute is glorified, and not one superseded no, nor so much as clouded.[18]

The only way God could show his justice and mercy in perfect harmony, without destroying the integrity of either, was through the propitiatory sacrifice of Christ. Merely forgiving, or doing away with sin, without the due punishment being dealt with, would not have maintained the integrity of God's character. Such thinking is echoed in Wesley's understanding of what the Old Testament teaches about the atonement. Of the 'mercy seat', the covering of the ark in Exodus 25:17–18, John Wesley commented: 'This propitiatory covering, as it might well be translated, was a type of Christ the great propitiation, whose satisfaction covers our transgressions, and comes between us and the curse we deserve.' He also contemplated the awesome nature of what is foreshadowed by the mercy seat: above it are the cherubim, facing each other, but looking downwards towards it. Here is depicted the longing of the angels of glory 'to look into the mysteries of the gospel, which they diligently contemplate, 1 Peter 1:12.'[19] Wesley correctly showed that here we are handling deep mysteries. We should tread carefully and reverentially, for we have entered into the holiest place.

---

18 J. Wesley, *Explanatory Notes Upon the New Testament,* Vol. II (London: 1813), notes on Romans 3:25–26.

19 J. Wesley, *Explanatory Notes Upon the Old Testament,* 1765, notes on Exodus 25:17–18.

The teaching of penal substitution was, to John Wesley, absolutely fundamental to Christianity. When Andrew Ramsay in his *Principles of Religion* rejected the view that the death of Christ was designed 'to appease vindictive justice and avert divine vengeance' as 'frivolous and blasphemous notions', Wesley objected strongly:

These 'frivolous and blasphemous notions' do I receive as the precious truths of God. And so deplorable is my ignorance, that I verily believe all who deny them, deny the Lord that bought them.[20]

Early in his life, John Wesley had found the writings of William Law helpful. However, in 1756 Wesley protested over the denial of the doctrine of justification by faith contained in some of Law's later statements, such as: 'There is no wrath in God, no fictitious atonement, no folly of debtor and creditor.' To counter what Law had written, Wesley quoted an unnamed sixteenth century author:

As man owed his Creator the perfect obedience of his whole life, or a punishment proportioned to his transgression, it was impossible he could satisfy him by a partial and imperfect obedience ... There was need, therefore, of a Mediator who could repair the immense wrong he had done to the Divine Majesty, satisfy the Supreme Judge, who had pronounced the sentence of death against the transgressions of His law, suffer in the place of His people, and merit for them pardon, holiness, and glory.

Yet, for Wesley, the propitiatory work of Christ was no cold, legal transaction—it was the 'inmost mystery of the Christian faith.' It was the supreme proof of the love of God, and came through 'the grace of the Son, who freely took our curse upon him, and imparts His blessing and merits to us.' The propitiatory death of the Saviour was no personal act of violence inflicted on him by the Father: it was an act of free, willing, loving submission within the Trinity in which Father, Son and Holy Spirit

---

20 **J. Wesley,** *Letters of John Wesley,* Vol. III (London: 1931), p. 109. Letter to Dr John Robertson 24 September 1753.

were at one. Wesley amplifies by reference to Isaiah 53. Although mankind had forsaken God, and so was liable to the highest punishment, 'The Mediator voluntarily interposed himself between them and the just Judge. And the incomprehensible love of God, that he might spare them, "spared not his own Son". ... "The Lord has laid on him the iniquity of us all".'[21]

AFTER THE WESLEYS

The same emphasis remained strong in the next generation of Wesley's followers. The eminent Methodist scholar and commentator Adam Clarke (c. 1762–1832), took up the strain. Commenting on Romans 3:25–27, he explained the way of salvation: 'Faith alone, in the mercy of God, through the propitiation made by the blood of Jesus is that, by which you can be justified, pardoned and taken into the Divine favour.'[22] Similarly, when dealing with the words of Isaiah 53:6, 'The Lord hath laid on him the iniquity of us all', Clarke's comments are unambiguous:

He was the subject on which all the rays collected on the focal point fell. These fiery rays, which should have fallen on all mankind, diverged from Divine justice to the east, west, north, and south, were deflected from them, and converged in Him. So the Lord hath caused to meet in Him the punishment due to the iniquities of ALL.[23]

To the Anglican, Thomas Scott (1747–1821), well known for his biblical commentary, the completeness of the atonement was crucial: 'Christ indeed bore the sins of all who should ever believe, in all their guilt, condemnation, and deserved punishment, in his body on the tree.'[24]

Eighteenth century evangelicals also consistently linked the teaching of

21 **J. Wesley,** *Letters of John Wesley,* Vol. III (London: 1931), pp.353–56.

22 **A. Clarke,** *The New Testament, With a Commentary and Critical Notes* (London: 1817), Romans 3.

23 **A Clarke,** *Commentary on the Old Testament* (London: 1825), Isaiah 53.

24 **T. Scott,** *The Force of Truth* (repr. Edinburgh: Banner of Truth, 1984), p. 65, quoted in **D. Bebbington,** *Evangelicalism in Modern Britain* (London: Unwin Hyman, 1989), pp. 15–16.

the cross, to the life of Christian duty and holiness. As Henry Venn (1724–1797) wrote, 'All treatises written to promote holiness must be deplorably defective, unless the cross of Christ be laid as the foundation.'[25] This link between the atonement and practical righteousness was continued into the nineteenth century.

The teaching of John Wesley, repeated in the work of Adam Clarke and others, became foundational to the army of lay preachers and class leaders who were the key players in the local Methodist circuits and societies. One such circuit was that around the Shropshire town of Madeley, the scene of the faithful ministry of John Fletcher (1729–1785) who was for a time the right-hand man of Wesley. Manuscripts from some of the sermons of these lay preachers still exist. They show how cross-centred was the Methodist lay preaching of the late eighteenth and early nineteenth centuries, and the way in which the atonement was understood. As one preacher, using Romans 3:25 as a text, expressed it:

A Propitiation means an atoning sacrifice, by which the Wrath of God is appeased. But how did He become this propitiation? I answer, by putting Himself in our Place, and drinking the Cup of Justice due to our sins.

Then, referring to Romans 8 'God spared not his own son …', the preacher amplified the theme: 'He spared Him not—But laid the whole weight of vindictive justice on His sacred Head—and He valiently [sic] accepted the dreadful Task.' The cost, the preacher emphasised, was awful and immense, 'He must drink the whole cup to the very Dregs—that He might become in the fullest sense our Propitiation.'

The challenges to love and obedience that flowed naturally from such an understanding were strongly expressed:

How cold are our returns of love to him who hath given Himself to bear our curse and suffer all our punishment … Here is the foundation of all our Blessings. The Saviour

---

25 **H. Venn,** *The Complete Duty of Man. 3rd.* edn. London 1779, p. xiii, quoted in **Bebbington,** *Evangelicalism in Modern Britain,* p. 16.

hath put himself in our place and born all the curse due to our sins ... He is at once our atonement and our righteousness.[26]

Not only did the early Methodists delight to preach the cross, they loved to sing its story. In singing of the saving work of Christ, the language of 'penal substitution' was never far away—

For what you have done
His blood must atone:
The Father hath punished for you his dear son,
The Lord, in the day
Of his anger, did lay
Your sins on the Lamb, and he bore them away.[27]

Or again:

Accomplished is the sacrifice,
The great redeeming work is done;
'Tis finished! All the debt is paid;
Justice divine is satisfied;
The grand and full atonement made;
God for a guilty world hath died.[28]

This awesome message these lay preachers gladly sang, and earnestly shared. They proclaimed it to the agricultural workers, the colliers, the tradespeople, of Madeley and the growing industrial Black Country. They and countless other Methodists across England preached what they had learned from Wesley, and Fletcher and Clarke, but more than that, they proclaimed the fruits of their plain reading of the Bible, which echoed with their personal experience. This evangelical message, with penal

---

26 Sermons 'Propitiation' in Names of Christ Collection, and 'Quickeneth' in Names of the Church Collection, manuscripts in John Rylands Library, Manchester.

27 C. Wesley, 'All ye that pass by', Hymn no. 707 in *Wesley's Hymns* (London: 1876).

28 C. Wesley, ''Tis finished, the Messias dies,' No 706 in *Wesley's Hymns,* 1876 edition.

substitution at its core, was spiritually liberating, and propelled them out into barns and cottages and kitchens, to tell what God had done through Christ for them. Their sermons brought comfort in distressing and troubled times, and secure hope of an eternal future with Christ. Such preaching filled Methodist chapels and class meetings: many ordinary, hurting, struggling, needy people heard it gladly, and countless lives were changed through its message.

The atonement in the nineteenth century

'In my place condemned he stood'[1]

The nineteenth century proved to be a most important, indeed pivotal, period in development of teaching upon the atonement. Ideas that had previously been seen as unorthodox and had been clearly rejected by the church as a whole, now began to be promoted by individuals within mainstream churches. By the end of the century they were gaining in popularity, as liberal theology became more widespread, and all who stood against such trends began to encounter resistance.

Those who owed a spiritual debt to the work of the eighteenth century Evangelical Revival maintained the pattern of teaching in which they had been nurtured.

CHARLES SIMEON

Charles Simeon (1759–1836) was to play a crucial role in the development of evangelicalism within the Church of England, at a time when it faced much opposition. His conversion came when, as a student, he prepared himself to attend a communion service in the college chapel. As he reflected on the Old Testament ideas of the transference of sin and guilt to the sacrifice, or the scapegoat in the Day of Atonement ceremony, he realised that he could be free of his sin and guilt by laying them on the sacred head of Jesus. This realisation of the substitutionary nature of the death of Christ brought rejoicing: 'At the Lord's Table in our chapel I had the sweetest access to God through my blessed Saviour.'[2]

---

1 From the hymn by **P. Bliss,** 'Man of Sorrows, What a Name!'
2 **W. Carus,** *Memoirs of the Life of the Rev. Charles Simeon*, London 1847. p. 9.

The apostle Paul's determination to know 'nothing but Jesus Christ and him crucified' (1 Corinthians 2:12) became central to Simeon's preaching.[3] All other teachings were to be judged by the relation they bore to two 'principle' doctrines: 'The lost state of man by nature, and his recovery through the blood of Christ.'[4] In the cross, the love and justice of God come together: 'If God had forgiven sins without any atonement, his justice to say the least would have lain concealed; perhaps, we may say, would have been greatly dishonoured.' God would have been perfectly just to consign sinners 'to everlasting perdition,' but instead, to satisfy the demands of his justice:

God sent his only dear Son, and lays on him our iniquities, and exacts of *him* the utmost farthing of our debt, then indeed the justice of God is 'declared', yea is exhibited in the most awful colours ... in the death of God's co-equal, co-eternal Son.

Simeon stressed the need personally to appropriate this atoning death: 'Let all then look to Christ as their all-sufficient propitiation, and to God as both "a just God and a Saviour." Then they shall find "that God is faithful, and *just* to forgive them their sins", yea, is "just in justifying all that believe."' Unbelievers, who do not place their faith in Christ, will themselves have to face what he faced upon the cross, for on the last day 'mercy will not have a word to say in arrest of judgement.'[5]

To Simeon, Isaiah 53 showed not only how Christ bears 'our sins in his own body on the tree,' but also the 'guilt of them, and the curse due to them.' Nothing less than this sacrifice could 'satisfy the demands of divine justice.' He depicts the Son calling out to the Father in voluntary and substitutionary fashion, 'inflict their punishment on me, and let them go free.'[6] Ideas of transference of sin and guilt, so important in his conversion, recur throughout Simeon's discussion: the 'mass of iniquity that had

---

3 **C. Simeon,** *Horae Homileticae: Expository Outlines on the Whole Bible* (1833, reprinted, Grand Rapids: Zondervan, 1951), Vol. 16. pp.40–41.

4 **Simeon,** *Expository Outlines,* Vol. 8, on Isaiah 53: 4–5. pp. 359–60.

5 **Simeon,** *Expository Outlines,* Vol. 15, No. 1833, on Romans 3:24–26. pp. 80–83.

6 **Simeon,** *Expository Outlines,* Vol. 8, Outline, 968 on Isaiah 53:4–5. pp. 356–57.

accumulated from the beginning to the end of time' was laid on Christ, so that 'having borne the curse due to them, he might take them all away from us forever.' The death of Christ, to Simeon, is a 'full perfect and sufficient propitiation' for sins.[7]

As he expounded his way through Scripture, Simeon was prepared to explore the rich range of ways used to describe the mystery of the atonement. On Mark 10:45, he showed how Christ's death was a ransom, his blood is 'the price paid for our redemption.' He saw Christ as the supreme example, the 'pattern of all that is great and glorious; a patience invisible, a love that passes the comprehension of either men or angels.' To this, asserted Simeon, 'we must look as to the pattern to which we are to be conformed.' However, he did not stop there, as others had done. Although the cross is the supreme demonstration of the love of Christ, through it atonement was objectively achieved. In this atonement believers must trust 'for our reconciliation to God.'[8]

WILLIAM WILBERFORCE

It has been claimed that those who understand the atonement of Christ as a work of penal substitution are weak in their social concern, and that the teaching lacks moral force.[9] The evidence of Christian history does not support such an assertion. Both Luther and Calvin had a strong social dimension to their teaching and practice. John Wesley, so strong in his arguments in favour of the penal and substitutionary death of Christ, was a man of deep social concern who worked zealously in support of the poor, and spoke out strongly against slavery, and the slave trade.

The most famous campaigner against the slave trade was William Wilberforce (1759–1833), a gentle, delightful man, filled with fun. He was converted at the age of twenty-five when an aspiring young MP with a

---

7 **Simeon,** *Expository Outlines*, Vol. 8, Outline 969 on Isaiah 53:6. pp. 363; and Outline 970 on Isaiah 53:7, p. 369.

8 **Simeon,** *Expository Outlines*, Vol. 12, Outline 1443 on Mark 10:45, p. 120.

9 **J.B. Green,** *Recovering the Scandal of the Cross: Atonement in New Testament and Contemporary Contexts* (Carlisle: Paternoster, 2003), p. 108.

career in Cabinet at his feet. Instead he played a strategic role in the campaigns to abolish the slave trade, and slavery in the British colonies, and he and his associates were outstanding for their humanitarian concern. Alongside his great benevolent projects, Wilberforce did all he could to promote the gospel through support for overseas and home mission. His *Practical View of Christianity* was written to challenge the formal, nominal Christianity that so prevailed amongst the affluent and privileged classes with whom he associated, and to urge upon his readers genuine, personal faith in Christ. To Wilberforce, the cross demonstrated both the love of God, and the reality of the 'guilt of sin', and how 'hateful it must be to the perfect holiness' of God. The justice of God required that a price for sin must be paid, and that: 'rather than sin should go unpunished, "God spared not his own Son"'; he was '"pleased to bruise him, and put him to grief," for our sakes.'

There is no doubt that Wilberforce saw Christ as a substitute for sinners, who:

Consented to take upon him our degraded nature, with all its weaknesses and infirmities; to be a 'man of sorrows;' 'to hide not his face from shame and spitting;' 'to be wounded for our transgressions, and bruised for our iniquities;' and at length to endure the sharpness of death, 'even the death of the cross;' that he might deliver us from the 'wrath to come;' and open the kingdom of heaven to all believers.

To Wilberforce, this 'wonderful transaction'—the atoning death of Christ—should drive people to be sure that they are right with God: 'This is a great challenge to unbelievers, who cannot escape "vengeance from heaven" against sin.' What Christ has achieved is also designed to provide a moral impetus to believers, giving 'an abiding disposition to please our great Benefactor; and … an humble persuasion that the weakest endeavours of this nature will not be despised by a Being who has already proved himself so kindly-affected towards us.'[10] Such profound reflections

---

10 **W. Wilberforce,** A Practical View of the Prevailing Religious System of Professed Christians, (1797, reprinted London: 1886), p. 259–260.

upon the cross made Wilberforce a moral reformer of immense significance.

Lest this interpretation of the cross be dismissed as exclusively white, Western, middle or upper class, reference should be made to the black African slave, Olaudah Equiano (1745–97) who was able to purchase his freedom. Through reading Acts 4:12, 'Salvation is found in no-one else', he was converted, and declared: 'I saw the Lord Jesus Christ in his humiliation, loaded, and bearing my reproach, sin, and shame.'[11] Whether slave, former slave, or friend of slaves, coming to see Christ as the substitute for sinners, who had borne guilt and condemnation, was life transforming.

JAMES AND ROBERT HALDANE

The itinerant ministries of James Haldane (1768–1851) and his brother Robert (1764–1842), did much to promote evangelicalism in Scotland, and led to the founding of many Congregational and Baptist churches. Robert Haldane was also instrumental in a small spiritual awakening in Geneva, during a period of preaching there in 1816. He later produced a commentary on Romans, based upon his lectures to Genevan students. He emphasised the centrality of justification by faith, the seriousness of sin, and the absolute demands of the justice of a holy God. These demands are met only in Christ:

Sin, as committed against God, is an infinite evil, and requires an infinite punishment; which cannot be borne in any limited time by those who are not capable of suffering punishment in an infinite degree. But the sufferings, as well as the obedience, in time, of Him who is infinite, are equivalent to the eternal obedience and sufferings of those who are finite … the infinite value of the death of the Redeemer equals an infinite number of finite punishments.

It was the Son of God who bore the 'equivalent to the eternal punishment of

---

11 **O. Equiano,** *The Interesting Narrative of the Life of Olaudah Equiano, or Gustavus Vassa, the African, Written by Himself* (1789).

those who had sinned.'[12] The propitiatory death of Christ dealt with the 'wrath of God for sins,' and satisfied 'the demands of His law and justice,' removing 'every obstruction to the exercise of His mercy towards them.' As with other evangelicals, Haldane emphasised the need for personal 'faith' in the atoning work of Christ: 'And this becomes a propitiation to us through faith in His blood—that is, when we believe that His death is a sacrifice which makes atonement for us, and when we rest on it as a sufficient answer to all accusations against us of the law of God.'[13]

ROBERT MURRAY MCCHEYNE

The well-crafted sermons of another Scotsman, Robert Murray McCheyne (1813–1843), are marked by their earnest evangelistic desire. The last sermon he ever preached in St Peter's, Dundee, before his untimely death, dealt with God's sovereignty and judgement. He set out examples of where God poured out his wrath, the supreme example of which was the cross:

So glorious, as an exhibition of God's justice, that the universe never saw its 'marrow'. 'Yet it pleased the Lord to bruise him'. These words do not give the least shadow of his suffering from God on account of our sin. Brethren, if any thing in the world can show that God will punish sin, it was the death of his dear and sinless Son.[14]

NINETEENTH CENTURY REVIVALISM

A development away from the classic revival of the eighteenth century was the emergence of revivalism, with an emphasis on the application of certain methods to achieve results, which were believed to be similar to revival. An important, and controversial, figure in promoting revivalism was Charles G. Finney (1792–1875), an American evangelist who had seen considerable success through his preaching. His sermons and writings

---

12 R. Haldane, *Exposition of the Epistle to the Romans* (reprinted London: Banner of Truth, 1958), p. 134.

13 Haldane, *Exposition of the Epistle to the Romans*, p. 150.

14 R.M. McCheyne, 'The Vessels to Wrath Fitted to Destruction', in *Sermons of Robert Murray McCheyne* (Edinburgh: Banner of Truth, 1961), pp. 182–83.

reveal a mixture of Abelard's moral influence, and later governmental, theories of the atonement. The cross, which demonstrates the supreme love of God, and is an incentive to the moral life, was necessary to maintain the moral government of God in the universe: 'Public justice, by which every executive magistrate in the universe is bound, sternly and peremptorily forbids that mercy shall be extended to any culprit ... without something being done that will fully answer as a substitute for the execution of penalties.'[15] The vicarious death of Christ maintains God's justice, and allows him to be both just and to forgive sin.[16] However, Finney found it hard to accept that on the cross Christ suffered an exact amount of eternal punishment to match the full eternal weight of the punishment due for sinners. Instead he bore a 'substitute for the curse,' as God 'commutes ... the sufferings of Christ for the damnation of men.'[17] Nonetheless, Finney still believed that the death of Christ was both substitutionary, and penal:

He stood in our stead where we must else have stood as condemned and quailing rebels; He suffered in His own person that awful manifestation of divine displeasure which would else have been made in our destruction in order to render it possible for God to be just to His government and good to all His subjects and yet pardon sinners.[18]

The American evangelist D.L. Moody (1837–1899) operated within this revivalist tradition, and became a major figure in American and British evangelicalism in the later nineteenth century. Moody had no theological training, and doctrinal precision in his statements was not his strong suit.

---

15 C. Finney, Lectures on Systematic Theology (1878, reprinted. California: Whittier, Kemp, 1944), pp. 264.

16 Finney, Systematic Theology, pp. 266, 271.

17 C. Finney, Skeletons of a Course of Theological Lectures, Manchester, S. Johnson and Son, 1845, Lectures 37: 4,4; 37: 7, 5, pp.253 and 257.

18 C. Finney, 'Substitution', Sermon on 2 Corinthians 5, 21, in Sermon Finney Collection, Vol. I, in Master Christian Library, Version 5, CD ROM, 1997.

One of his major biographers believes Moody's preaching on the cross was the moral influence teaching, stressing the love of Christ which melts the heart and brings the prodigal home.[19] However, the evidence of Moody's sermons suggests he especially saw the cross in penal and substitutionary terms; indeed he declared: 'I would rather give up my life than give up this doctrine.'[20] In his sermon 'The Blood', he explains: 'Sin entered and brought death into the world … I must either die, or get someone to die for me; and in the fullness of time Christ comes forward to die for the sinner.' Christ is the 'sinner's only hope of heaven, and the sinner's only substitute.' Again and again Moody turned the message of the cross into one of evangelistic challenge: 'God says "There is the Blood; it is all I have to give … I am satisfied with the finished work of my Son, and will you be satisfied?" Don't leave this meeting until you claim this as yours.'[21]

To Moody, salvation comes through faith in the substitutionary death of Christ: 'The moment I believe in the Lord Jesus Christ as my substitute, as my Saviour, that moment I get life and peace.' The cross deals with the problem of sin: 'The penalty, the wages of sin is death. Christ received the wages on Calvary, and therefore there is no condemnation.'[22] His certainty on this point was striking: 'Take the doctrine of substitution out of my Bible, and I would not take it home with me tonight.'[23] Substitution involves bearing the debt of condemnation:

It is as if he owed someone a debt, and when he went to pay it, was told, 'There is nothing against you; it is all settled' … 'someone else has come and paid it.' That is substitution. Now I know who paid my spiritual debt, it was the Lord Jesus Christ.[24]

19 J.F. Findlay, *Dwight L. Moody* (Chicago: University of Chicago Press, 1969), pp. 232–236

20 D.L. Moody, 'The Blood', in *Wondrous Love: Sermons by D.L.Moody* (1876, reprinted, London: Pickering and Inglis, n.d.), p. 65.

21 D.L. Moody, 'The Blood', pp. 53, 64–5, 68.

22 D.L. Moody, 'One Word—Gospel', in *Wondrous Love*, pp. 113, 115.

23 D.L. Moody, 'Tracing the Scarlet Thread', in *New Sermons, Addresses and Prayers* (Chicago: Goodspeed, 1877), p. 154.

24 D.L. Moody, 'The Blood, Part II', in *Twelve Select Sermons* (Chicago: 1880). p. 110.

Moody then used a striking illustration which revealed that he had no doubt that Christ's death was both substitutionary and penal. He pictured a man confronted by a blazing prairie fire racing towards him. He is unable to outrun the flames, so what does he do? He takes out a match and burns a patch of grass around where he stands. When the flames come, they pass by where he stands, because the ground has already been burned over, there is nothing flammable left. In the same way, the atoning death of Christ deals with the wrath of God against sin:

There is one mountain peak that the wrath of God has swept over—that is Mount Calvary, and that fire swept its fury upon the bosom of the Son of God. Take your stand here by the cross, and you will be safe for time and eternity. Escape for your life; flee to yon mountain, and you are saved this very minute.[25]

C.H. SPURGEON

One of those who welcomed Moody's directness in proclaiming the gospel, was the great preacher and evangelist, Charles Haddon Spurgeon (1834–1892). To him also, the cross was absolutely fundamental: 'Take away this substitutionary death of our Lord, and you have taken all away.'[26] Because 'we are made nigh by the blood of Christ,' this is the 'first, the grandest, the highest, the most essential truth' for us to preach:

God is glorified because Christ was punished for the sin of his people ... On the cross we see sin fully punished and yet fully pardoned. We see justice with her gleaming sword triumphant, and mercy with her silver sceptre regnant in sublimest splendour. Glory be to the wondrous wisdom which discovered the way of blending vengeance with love, making a tender heart to be the mirror of unflinching severity, causing the crystal vase of Jesus' loving nature to be filled with the red wine of righteous wrath.[27]

---

25 **Moody,** 'One Word—Gospel'. p. 120.

26 **C.H. Spurgeon,** 'Slaying the Sacrifice', Sermon Preached at Metropolitan Tabernacle, 23 March 1884, in *Spurgeon's Expository Encyclopaedia*, Vol. 1 (reprinted 1984), p. 345.

27 **C.H. Spurgeon,** 'Nearness to God', Sermon Preached at Metropolitan Tabernacle, 17 Jan 1869, *Expository Encyclopaedia*, Vol. 1, pp. 330–331.

Although the cross was the main focus of Spurgeon's preaching, he did not confine the atoning sufferings of Christ solely to Calvary. Spurgeon saw in Gethsemane that the great and crushing weight of sin Christ was to bear as substitute was already resting upon him, and when he was cruelly scourged by Pilate's soldiers.[28] But then, on the cross: 'The whole of the punishment of his people was distilled into one cup, "At one tremendous draught of love, He drank damnation dry." He drank all, endured all, suffered all.'[29] This truth was to be understood and applied in personal terms, as sin is punished and the justice of God is satisfied:

He was there, on the cross, in our room and place, and stead … Jesus Christ, standing in the place of the sinner, and enduring that which would vindicate the justice of God, had to come under the cloud, as the sinner must have come, if Christ had not taken his place.[30]

In this work the Father and the Son were absolutely at one: 'There was no divided purpose; they went both of them together … "God so loved the world that he gave his only-begotten Son;" but Jesus so loved the world that he gave himself. The atonement was the gift of the Father; but it was the work of the Son …'[31]

Spurgeon became deeply alarmed at hearing of sermons with very little of the cross in them, and at those who began to question the traditional understanding of the atonement. He was appalled at modern theories of the atonement which said little more than: 'Jesus Christ did something or

---

28 C.H. Spurgeon, 'Christ in Gethsemane', Preached at Metropolitan Tabernacle, 1 June 1879, *Expository Encyclopaedia*, Vol. 4 (reprinted 1984), p. 246.

29 C.H. Spurgeon, 'Justification by Grace', Sermon Preached at the Music Hall, Royal Surrey Gardens, London, 5 April 1857, section 1. See also 'Particular Redemption', Sermon Preached at Music Hall, Royal Surrey Gardens, 28 February 1858, Section 3.

30 C.H. Spurgeon, 'The Saddest Cry from the Cross', Sermon Preached at Metropolitan Tabernacle, 7 January, 1877, in *Expository Encyclopaedia*, Vol. 4, p. 321.

31 C.H. Spurgeon, 'Alone, Yet *Not* Alone', Sermon Preached at Metropolitan Tabernacle, 2 March 1890, in *Expository Encyclopaedia*, Vol. 4, p. 238.

other, which, in some way or other, was, in some degree or other, connected with our salvation.' He wanted to speak of the 'fact' of the atonement, not merely debate 'theories' of the atonement. Different gospels, which 'leave out the great central truth of substitution', were of little use to the masses, and were profoundly unsafe: 'Do not try to go beyond the gospel, brethren; you will get into the mud if you do.' Spurgeon urged his hearers to stand firm upon the truth of the gospel: 'It is safe standing here; and standing here I can comprehend how our Lord Jesus took the sinner's place, and passing under the sentence which the sinner deserved ...could cry "My God, my God, why hast thou forsaken me?"'[32]

Unless Christ had borne the punishment of sin, then the human race was destined to face eternal condemnation. With this stark prospect in view, Spurgeon challenged the shift in doctrinal standards amongst those who professed to be evangelicals, and the rapid ground being made by theological liberalism, in what became known as the 'Downgrade Controversy.'

Challenges from the rise of liberal theology

FRIEDRICH SCHLEIERMACHER

Questioning traditional teaching about the cross was not original to the nineteenth century, but the extent and pervasiveness of it was new. What had previously only been promoted by those who denied other fundamental doctrines, such as Socinus, was now embraced by figures of influence within mainstream Christianity. The German theologian Friedrich Schleiermacher (1768–1834), reacting against the Enlightenment stress on rationality and the intellect, saw that religion was more to do with the heart, than the head; the feelings, rather than the mind. He had little to say about sin—it was more a problem to man than to God. He dismissed views that made the forgiveness of sin dependent 'upon the punishment which Christ suffered' as 'magical',[33] and the wrath of God as an 'obscure

---

32 **C.H. Spurgeon,** 'The Saddest Cry from the Cross', p. 322.
33 **F.D.E. Schleiermacher,** The Christian Faith, p. 435, in McDonald, Atonement, p. 213.

illusion'. The only connection between the forgiveness of sins and Christ's sufferings comes in his showing sympathy and understanding with the human condition. Schleiermacher thus reduced the cross to being merely an inspiration to the spiritually weak, rather than a full work of atonement for those who are spiritually guilty, lost, and under the condemnation of God. The resurrection, ascension, and return of Christ are rendered of little significance.

This was radical indeed. As dean of the theological faculty, and later Rector of Berlin University, he was well positioned to promote his views. Schleiermacher has been called the founder of modern theology, and his teaching was extremely influential in the development of liberal theology, at the heart of which is radical doubt about the cross. Reinhold Niebuhr was later to neatly sum up the teaching of liberal theology as follows: 'A God without wrath brought men without sin into a kingdom without judgement through the ministration of a Christ without a cross.'[34]

HORACE BUSHNELL

One Congregationalist minister in mid-nineteenth century America, Horace Bushnell (1802–1876), was deeply influenced by reading Schleiermacher, and has been called the father of American religious liberalism. He depicted Christ as 'the moral power of God', who through the incarnation entered into the lot of mankind, and served, and healed, and sympathised, and suffered. The cross was the greatest display of the goodness of love, revealing the pain endured by the eternal heart of God because of sin, but Bushnell denied that there was any necessity for 'penal satisfaction', or compensation to 'God's justice for the release of transgression.' Instead, he believed that the cross was designed to awaken in humans a response to God's love, of repentance and changed life. It is this change in us that propitiates God,[35] but the cross was not in itself an atonement for sin.

---

34 Quoted in **A. Lane,** *The Lion Concise Book of Christian Thought* (Tring: Lion, 1984), p. 173.

35 **H. Bushnell,** *The Vicarious Sacrifice* (London: Strahan, 1866), pp. 126, 217, 450. Bushnell later modified his views in *Forgiveness and Law* (1874), in which he was even prepared to use the word 'propitiation'.

JOHN MCLEOD CAMPBELL

In early nineteenth-century Britain some began to express radical doubts about traditional understandings of the atonement. One such was John McLeod Campbell (1800–72), a brilliant but controversial Church of Scotland minister who in 1830 was deposed for questioning the teaching of the Westminster Confession of Faith on limited atonement. After he became the minister of an independent church in Glasgow he continued to develop his views, which he subsequently published in his famous work *The Nature of the Atonement* (1856). He had influential friends, and his ideas, although contentious, began to spread. Campbell stressed that atonement is the work of a loving God—but so did advocates of penal substitution. He even accepted that the wrath of God against sin was a reality, but that instead of an equivalent punishment for human sin being required to make atonement, an equivalent sorrow or repentance for sin was sufficient, and was in fact 'the higher and more excellent' way.[36] Campbell argued that it was the 'spiritual essence' of the sufferings of Christ which gave them atoning value, 'not that these sufferings were penal.' In place of penal substitution, he spoke of substitutionary, or vicarious, repentance: Christ offers a 'perfect confession of our sins.'[37] On the cross, he did not suffer the punishment for sin, but showed the 'suffering of divine love caused by our sins.' Christ's repentance, Campbell believed, brings 'true and proper satisfaction to the offended justice' more than any idea of Christ bearing the penalty for sin: there is 'more atoning worth 'in one tear of true and perfect sorrow' than in 'endless ages of penal sorrow.'[38]

Whilst the work of Campbell is undoubtedly moving, it leaves huge questions. If all that God required was a work of true repentance, why did Christ need to go to the cross, why was the agony in Gethsemane not sufficient? The physical and spiritual sufferings, so clearly depicted in

---

36 J. McLeod Campbell, *The Nature of the Atonement, and its Relation to Remission of Sins and Eternal Life* (James Clarke, 1856, 7th edition, reprinted London: 1959), pp. 135, 137.

37 Campbell, *The Nature of the Atonement*, pp. 118–119, 135.

38 Campbell, *The Nature of the Atonement*, pp. 140–41, 145–6.

Scripture as part of Christ's giving of his total self, serve no real purpose in Campbell's scheme. It also remains unclear how vicarious repentance satisfies the justice of God. How can Christ offer perfect repentance and confession, when he himself knew no sin? Repentance is a response to personal consciousness of sin, and it seems artificial to speak of someone repenting and confessing in the place of another. Another cannot repent on the part of the prodigal—he must do this himself. The substitutionary sacrifices of the Old Testament foreshadow that of Christ, but if Campbell's scheme is followed, how can an animal sacrifice repent on behalf of the sinner making the sacrifice, or point to the perfect repentance Christ was to supposed to have offered?

A CONGREGATIONALIST RESPONSE

R.W. Dale, the Congregationalist minister of Carrs Lane Chapel in Birmingham, attempted to challenge such new thinking. Although not entirely conservative in all his theology, and somewhat inclined to the view that the death of Christ was a penal example, in his work *The Atonement* (1875) Dale still included many statements about the cross that were clearly both penal and substitutionary. He maintained that huge portions of the Scripture would lose their significance if they were not understood in this way. Sin is a transgression of God's law, and demands punishment. Christ, as the moral ruler of the universe, is the one who must punish sin, but 'instead of inflicting the penalties, [he] has submitted to them; he has "died the just for the unjust", and has been made a curse for us.'[39] This is the awesome marvel of the atonement, more than simply a moving spectacle, or a mere act of sympathy with us. Dale was categorical in his understanding that the death of Christ was propitiatory: 'The ground on which God cancels human guilt, and delivers the guilty from "the wrath" which threatened them.' In the cross, Christ truly bears the punishment of sin: 'He was forsaken of God, that we might not have to be forsaken. He did not suffer that he might merely share with us the penalties of our sin, but that the penalties of sin might be remitted.'[40]

---

39 R.W. Dale, *The Atonement* (London: Hodder and Stoughton, 1878), p. 422.

40 Dale, *The Atonement,* pp. 236, 433.

THE EVANGELICAL RESPONSE—THE HODGES

Amongst American defenders of the view that the atonement was a work of penal substitution, Charles Hodge (1797–1878) stands as a notable example. He worked at Princeton Seminary from 1820 in changing and troubled times, as the orthodox Calvinism of the Westminster Confession came under challenge, and liberal theology advanced in the middle and later parts of the nineteenth century. Hodge's *Systematic Theology* (1872–73) encapsulates his defence of orthodox teaching, including his re-statement of the traditional view of penal substitution. Hodge argued that justice was a part of God's essential nature, and therefore it was appropriate to use the language of the law courts in speaking of the atonement. Sin can only be pardoned 'in consistency with the divine justice only on the ground of forensic penal satisfaction'. Scripture declares clearly:

The immutability of the divine law; the necessity of its demand being satisfied; the impossibility of sinners making that satisfaction for themselves; the possibility of it being rendered by substitution.[41]

Sin brings punishment, and only through the bearing of the punishment for sin can pardon be brought. Nothing else but the blood of Christ 'has power sufficient to atone.' However, to satisfy the demands of the law, mere punishment is not enough, all righteousness must be fulfilled. Therefore, Christ, 'by his obedience and sufferings, by his whole righteousness, active and passive, he, as our representative and substitute, did and endured all that the law demands.' This saving work of Christ, a 'wonderfully constituted person' is 'the great constituent principle of the religion of the Bible.'[42]

In his *Outlines of Theology*, Charles Hodge's son, Archibald (1823–1886), also emphasised the justice of God, whose eternal nature 'immutably determines him to punish all sin.' It is therefore absolutely

---

41 C. Hodge, *Systematic Theology*, Vol. II (London: 1871–73. Reprinted, London: James Clarke, 1960). pp. 488, 494.

42 C. Hodge, *Systematic Theology*, II, pp. 489, 494.

necessary for the law to be satisfied, and for there to be an atonement if God is to redeem and forgive sinners. The sufferings of Christ were therefore 'a strict penal satisfaction, the person suffering being a substitute.'[43] There must be no doubt that the penalty for sin has been fully paid: 'His sufferings were no substitute for a penalty, but … a full equivalent for all that was demanded of us.'[44]

Some believe that this emphasis upon justice gives the impression that God was somehow reluctant to bring forgiveness, but this is a misrepresentation. To Archibald Hodge, the supreme motive of God in the atonement was 'the amazing love of God to his own people, determining in perfect consistency with his truth and justice, to assume himself, in the person of his Son, the responsibility of bearing the penalty and satisfying justice.' Both Father and Son willingly agreed upon the atonement: 'The same identical attributes are common to the Father and the Son. The justice demanding satisfaction, and the love prompting the self-assumption of the penalty, are co-existent states of divine feeling and purpose.'[45] God's love is demonstrated in the atoning death of Christ, and this inspires the believer: 'Being an exhibition of amazing love … it effects what only such love can; it melts the heart, subdues the rebellion, and dissipates the fears of sinful men.'[46]

J.C. RYLE

To the Anglican evangelical J.C. Ryle (1816–1900), the suffering of Christ upon the cross is supremely demonstrated by the cry of dereliction (Matthew 27:46). It revealed, 'The real pressure on His soul of the enormous burden of a world's sins; they were meant to show how truly and literally he was our substitute—was made sin and a curse for us—and endured God's righteous anger against a world's sin in his own person.'[47]

---

43 A.A. Hodge, *Outlines of Theology* (London: Hodder and Stoughton, 1879. Reprinted Edinburgh: Banner of Truth), pp. 157, 405.

44 A.A. Hodge, *The Atonement* (London: Nelson and Sons, 1868), p. 29.

45 Hodge, *The Atonement,* p. 28.

46 Hodge, *The Atonement,* p. 30.

47 J.C. Ryle, *Expository Thoughts on the Gospels: Matthew,* (James Clarke, 1856. Reprinted Cambridge: 1974), p. 394.

In days when clarity and certainty in matters of doctrine have again gone out of fashion, Ryle's approach in defending penal substitution is instructive. Four years after he became Bishop of Liverpool, he lamented the rise of:

Jelly-fish Christianity—a Christianity without bone, or muscle, or sinew—without any distinct teaching about the atonement or the work of the Spirit, or justification, or the way of peace with God—a vague, foggy, misty Christianity, of which the only watchwords seem to be ... 'You must condemn no man's doctrinal views. You must consider everybody is right, and nobody is wrong'.[48]

Ryle made clear his belief that matters of eternal significance were at stake when discussing the atonement. The bishop declared his conviction that salvation was 'procured for us by His vicarious sacrifice, the deliverance from the guilt and power and consequences of sin, which He purchased when He suffered as our Substitute'. To Ryle, the spiritual destiny of the believer rested upon this: 'The thing that we all need to save us from eternal death is not merely Christ's incarnation and life, but Christ's *death*. The atoning "blood" which Christ shed when He died is the grand secret of salvation.' This alone could bring hope for eternity, as he solemnly warned: 'When you come to your deathbed, you will want something more than an example ... Take heed that you are found resting all your weight on Christ's substitution for you on the cross, and His atoning blood, or it will be better if you had never been born.'[49]

HYMNOLOGY

The substitutionary death of Christ remained a central theme in Christian hymn writing in the nineteenth century. The words of the hymns of Philip Bliss, and Thomas Kelly are typical of many other examples—

---

48 J.C. Ryle, 'One Blood', Sermon Preached at the Chapel Royal, St James's, London, March 2, 1884, in *The Upper Room: Being a Few Truths for the Times* (London: Wm Hunt, 1888. Reprinted Edinburgh: Banner of Truth, 1970), pp. 99.

49 Ryle, 'One Blood', pp. 98, 108.

Chapter 6

Bearing shame and scoffing rude,
In my place condemned he stood;
Sealed my pardon with his blood;
Hallelujah! What a Saviour![50]

Inscribed upon the cross we see,
In shining letters, 'God is love';
He bears our sins upon the tree;
And brings us mercy from above.[51]

LATE NINETEENTH-CENTURY VIEWS

The understanding of the death of Christ as a propitiatory sacrifice was not only held by evangelicals, but was still maintained across most Christian traditions. John Henry Newman (1801–1890), who moved from Anglo-Catholicism to Roman Catholicism, eventually becoming a cardinal, summed up his view of the substitutionary death of Christ in his hymn, 'Praise to the Holiest in the Height':

O Loving Wisdom of Our God,
When all was sin and shame,
A Second Adam to the Fight,
And to the Rescue Came …

O generous love! that He Who smote
In Man for man the foe,
The double agony in Man
For man should undergo.

Even those inclining to theological liberalism were still reverting to the traditional way of speaking of the atonement. *Lux Mundi*, a series of essays which appeared in 1889, caused great controversy over the liberal theological perspectives that it included. Yet the essay on the atonement,

---

50 From the hymn by **Philip Bliss** (1838–76), 'Man of Sorrows, What a Name!'
51 From the hymn by **Thomas Kelly** (1769–1854), 'We Sing the Praise of Him Who Died.'

whilst challenging the way some penal theories of substitution were expressed, still affirmed the truth of 'the wrath of God against sin, and the love of Christ by which that wrath was removed,' and that Christ's death was 'the expiation for those past sins which have laid the burden of guilt upon the human soul, and it is also the propitiation of the wrath of God.'[52]

The Dean of Canterbury, R.W. Farrar (1831–1903), also noted for his broad theological views, wrote in 1900 that 'the survival of doctrinal crudities, no longer tenable with the truths brought home to us by the light of advancing knowledge, is a *chief*, if it be not the sole, cause ... for widespread disbelief.' Yet for all his doubt as to past modes of expression, Farrar believed that although the atonement 'surpasses our powers of understanding', it was still a 'full, perfect and sufficient redemption, propitiation and satisfaction for all the sins of the whole world, both original and actual.' Farrar used Richard Hooker's words from the sixteenth century to summarise the kernel of the Christian message: 'We care for no knowledge in the world but this, that man hath sinned and God hath suffered; that God hath made himself the sin of men, and that men are made the righteousness of God'[53]

---

52 A. Lyttleton, 'The Atonement', in *Lux Mundi* (London: John Murray, 13th edition, 1892), pp. 209, 226.

53 R.W. Farrar in *The Atonement in Modern Religious Thought: A Theological Symposium* (London: James Clarke, 1900), pp. 34, 56–57.

The atonement in the twentieth century

'The Very Heart of the Christian Gospel'[1]

T he voices of those who in the nineteenth century began to oppose traditional teaching on the death of Christ as being a work of penal substitution became stronger in the early part of the twentieth. In the West, it was no longer deemed appropriate to a 'modern' audience to speak of ideas such as atonement and shedding blood, let alone punishment and wrath. The playwright and social commentator George Bernard Shaw declared, 'I detest the doctrine of the Atonement', and delivered his view that 'ladies and gentlemen cannot, as such, possibly allow anyone else to expiate their sins by suffering a cruel death.'[2] Those within the church became increasingly sensitive to such disapproving noises from outside, and sought to adjust the message. This owed much to the growing strength of liberal theology in many churches, and was associated with the questioning of other doctrines such as the authority of Scripture, and the deity of Christ. The connection between such huge theological changes, in a century of two world wars and enormous social conflict, and the steep decline in Christian adherence in Western Europe is unmistakable. In the face of such challenges, shifting from foundational teaching neither won over sceptics nor brought back non-attendees to church.

---

1 **J.I. Packer,** 'What did the Cross Achieve?: The Logic of Penal Substitution', *Tyndale Bulletin*, 25 (1974), reprinted in **J.I. Packer,** *Celebrating the Saving Work of God: The Collected Shorter Writings of J.I. Packer* (Carlisle: Paternoster, 1998), p. 86.

2 **G.B. Shaw,** 'What is My Religious Faith?' *Sixteen Self-Sketches.* London 1949. p. 79, in Bebbington, *Evangelicalism in Modern Britain.* p. 16.

DENNEY AND FORSYTH

At the start of the twentieth century, some valiantly attempted, against the rising tide of criticism, to defend the view that the atonement was a work of penal substitution. In 1903 the Scottish theologian James Denney argued that 'the death of Christ is the central thing in the New Testament';[3] without the atonement, there was no gospel. It is God's response to a profound problem: 'Sin in me is as deep as my being.'[4] Denney affirmed the 'naked fact' of the atonement, which is that 'Christ, by God's appointment, dies the sinner's death. The doom falls upon him, and is exhausted there.' This death is an act of genuine substitution—'What was our due, and not his, he made his; what we owed, and he did not, he paid.'[5] It was also a work of propitiation, as he bore our sins and the wrath of God fell on Christ: 'our punishment is transferred to Him, and the penal consequences of sin need not trouble us further.'[6]

Much is included in Denney's writing that is important and helpful. He does, however, hesitate over affirming that Christ bore an exact equivalent for the penalties against sin. This leaves a difficulty. Can believers rest completely secure that the full debt has been paid, that no further penalty remains, and that they are at peace with God?

Peter Taylor Forsyth was drawn as a young minister to liberal theology, and took part in the 1877 Leicester conference of Congregationalists which helped encourage such thinking. However, by the early twentieth century he found that the over-emphasis on the love of God in liberal theology ended with a sentimental concept of love, and he turned back to more traditional theological expressions. To Forsyth, the wrath of God was no less real than the love of God: God can express anger towards those he

---

3 **J. Denney,** *The Death of Christ,* revised edition (London: Hodder and Stoughton, 1911), p. 20.

4 **J. Denney,** *Studies in Theology* (3rd edn., London: Hodder and Stoughton, 1895), pp. 106, 112; and **J. Denney,** *The Christian Doctrine of Reconciliation* (London: Hodder and Stoughton, 1918), p. 195, quoted in McDonald, pp. 272–73.

5 **Denney,** *Death of Christ.* p. 277.

6 **Denney,** *Reconciliation.* p. 281, quoted in **McDonald,** p. 278.

loves. He made an important contribution by placing the holiness of God at the heart of the atonement; that alone can explain the desperate nature of humanity's problem: 'It is the holiness of God's love that necessitates the atoning cross.'[7] It creates the issues of sin and guilt, God's love is a holy love, and is therefore wrathful against sin:

There is a penalty and a curse for sin; and Christ consented to enter that region. Christ entered voluntarily into the pain and horror which is sin's penalty from God.[8]

In his holy death, Christ 'was made sin', and dealt with the judgement of God: 'in Christ, judgement becomes finished and final, because none but a holy Christ could spread sin out in all its sinfulness for thorough judgement.'[9] Forsyth's arguments are certainly complex, and at times unclear. On the one hand he rejects the idea of transference of sin and guilt from humanity to Christ: 'We have outgrown the idea that Christ took our sin's punishment in the quantitative sense of the word. What he offered was not an equivalent … but the due judgement of it, its condemnation'. 'It was not substitutionary punishment,' yet at the same time he affirmed that 'it was because of the world's sin that Christ suffered. It was the punishment of that sin that fell on Him.'[10] This suffering was the penalty in the moral order due to sin, and it brings humans to repentance and reconciliation. Undoubtedly, Forsyth had important things to say, and his recognition of the weakness of liberal theology is notable, but his explanation of the atonement needed a clearer expression of how Christ bears the full measure of the sin and guilt of mankind, and the punishment due against them.

THE ASCENDANCY OF LIBERAL THEOLOGY

Between the 1920s and the 1940s, liberal theology was in the ascendancy

---

7 **P.T. Forsyth,** *The Work of Christ* (London: Hodder and Stoughton, 1910), pp. 79–80.

8 **Forsyth,** *The Work of Christ,* p. 147.

9 **Forsyth,** *The Work of Christ,* p. 160.

10 **P.T. Forsyth,** Section III, in *The Atonement in Modern Religious Thought: A Theological Symposium* (London: James Clarke, 1900), pp. 65, 85.

within Protestantism, and profoundly shaped doctrinal pronouncements on the atonement. L.W. Grensted declared 'The penal theory is now extinct.' The New Testament scholar Vincent Taylor argued that 'St Paul does not hold a theory of vicarious punishment.'[11] Whilst he believed that the death of Christ upon the cross revealed God's judgement upon sin, and that in death he identified with humanity, and revealed horror for sin and its presence, he preferred to speak of the representative work of Christ, rather than his substitutionary work. Taylor, therefore, depicted Christ's death as 'the expression of his perfect penitence for the sins of men.'[12] Following MacLeod Campbell, he replaced vicarious punishment with vicarious repentance, with all its difficulties of a sinless Saviour repenting on behalf of sinners. Yet even Taylor struggled to maintain his distinction between representation and substitution in the light of the New Testament evidence, which, he is remarkably forced to concede, comes 'within a hair's breadth of substitution', and that 'the representative work of Christ is almost, but not quite, substitutionary'.[13] Other scholars were drawn to the moral influence theory of Peter Abelard, seeing the cross as a revelation of divine love, designed to produce a response of love and gratitude in sinners, rather than something that deals with the reality of their sin and guilt, and God's just response to that. Much of Western Protestantism came to accept teaching that had once been rejected as quite unorthodox by Protestant and Catholic alike.

THE TIDE BEGINS TO TURN

An attempt to return to earlier ways of thinking about the atonement was made by the Professor of Theology at the University of Lund in Sweden from 1913–33, Gustav Aulén. In *Christus Victor* he drew on writings from some early church theologians and Martin Luther, in which the atonement

---

11 V. Taylor, *The Atonement in the New Testament.* (London: Epworth, 1949), p. 127.

12 V. Taylor, *Jesus and His Sacrifice: A Study of the Passion-Sayings in the Gospels* (London: Macmillan, 1937), p. 309.

13 V. Taylor, *The Doctrine of the Atonement in the Light of New Testament Teaching.* (London: Epworth Press, 1940), pp. 288–289.

is spoken of as the victory of God in Christ over the evil forces in the world, which brings reconciliation between God and the world: 'It is precisely the work of salvation wherein Christ breaks the power of evil that *constitutes* the atonement between God and the world.' Although love triumphs in the defeat of the forces of evil, Aulén did not see any need for the 'satisfaction of God's justice.'[14]

Aulén certainly highlighted an important, and sometimes neglected, aspect of the work of Christ. However, the idea of 'victory' does not convey all that there is in Scripture about the atonement, either in the early church fathers or in Luther. Victory is the *result* of the work of the cross, where Christ deals decisively with sin and guilt and the righteous judgement of God against these. It is also unclear what Aulén actually means by the 'forces of evil', for he writes: 'In the New Testament we often meet more or less mythologically formulated expressions for this complex of evil powers.'[15] By this he seems to be referring to powers generated by human, collective sinfulness, which makes it difficult to understand what is entailed by the victory of Christ that Aulén describes. Nor does he say much about what it cost God to win this decisive victory upon the cross.

The dominant figure of Western Protestant theology of the twentieth century was the Swiss theologian Karl Barth. His neo-orthodox theology profoundly challenged the bankruptcy of liberal theology's exaltation of the thoughts of man above the revelation of God, and its failed emphasis on human progress and perfectability, which had been exposed in the light of the horrors of the First World War. Yet Barth's theology was not a return to conservative evangelicalism, and he did not set out any coherent or specific doctrine of the atonement. He saw it rather as a supremely divine miracle, which lies beyond the formulations of human reasoning. He did, however, use language which rejected radical liberal doubt, and appeared to be a return to traditional, substitutionary, ways of speaking of the cross: 'He

---

14 **G. Aulén,** *Christus Victor,* **trans. A.G. Herbert** (London: SPCK, 1931), pp. 87, 163.

15 **G. Aulén,** *The Faith of the Christian Church* (Muhlenberg Press: Philadelphia, 1948), p. 275 cited by **M.J. Ovey,** *Aulén Appropriated*, Paper at Evangelical Alliance Symposium, London School of Theology, July 2005.

has therefore suffered for all men what they had to suffer.' Jesus Christ not only bore 'man's enmity against God's grace, revealing it in all its depth', he also bore 'the far greater burden, the righteous wrath of God against those who are enemies of this grace, the wrath which must fall upon us.' In the cross, an amazing reversal takes place: 'The passion of Jesus Christ is the judgement of God, in which the Judge himself was the judged.'[16]

Clive Staples Lewis became a Christian after a long period of unbelief and scepticism. He was particularly troubled by the teaching of penal substitution, that 'God wanted to punish men for having deserted and joined the Great Rebel, but Christ volunteered to be punished instead.' After his conversion Lewis came to see that this understanding of the atonement no longer looked 'quite so immoral and so silly as it used to.'[17] His portrayal of the death and resurrection of Aslan on the great stone table in his children's story *The Lion, the Witch and the Wardrobe* clearly represents a substitutionary view of the atonement. After his restoration to life the great lion explains the 'magic deeper still', in which, 'when a willing victim who had committed no treachery was killed in a traitor's stead, the Table would crack and death would start working backwards.'[18]

MARTYN LLOYD-JONES

Although many had abandoned the traditional penal and substitutionary understanding of the atonement, evangelicals in the twentieth century continued to defend the teaching, and emphasise its place at the heart of the gospel. In this, an important role was played by Dr Martyn Lloyd-Jones, who ministered at Westminster Chapel, London, from 1938 to 1968. He worked hard to challenge the liberal ascendancy, expose the limitations of Barth's neo-orthodoxy, and consolidate evangelical theology, in part

---

16 **K. Barth,** *Church Dogmatics.* (Edinburgh: T&T Clark, 1956–57), Vol. 4, I. pp. 552–53; and Vol. 2, I. p. 152; Vol. 4, I. p. 254.

17 **C.S. Lewis,** *Mere Christianity* (Glasgow: Collins, 1977), p. 52.

18 **C.S. Lewis,** *The Lion, the Witch, and the Wardrobe*, in *The Complete Chronicles of Narnia* (1950, repr. London: HarperCollins, 1980), p. 148.

through a call to learn from the great teachers of the past, especially the Reformers and the Puritans. His careful, patient, expositions of Scripture became a model many others were to follow.

For Lloyd-Jones, the cross was 'the most tremendous, the most glorious, the most staggering thing in the universe and in the whole of history,' and Romans 3:25 was 'absolutely crucial for a true understanding of Christian doctrine and the way of salvation.'[19] Aware that many people were ridiculing the propitiatory nature of the death of Christ, declaring it as 'almost blasphemous to speak of the wrath of God,' he issued a challenge based on the evidence of Scripture: 'If you go through the Bible without theories and preconceived notions, you will see at once … that God is angry against sin, that God hates sin, that the wrath of God upon sin is taught everywhere and is a basic proposition.' In understanding the cross, foundational issues needed to be properly understood. The wrath of God, was not 'uncontrolled passion,' but 'His settled opposition to all that is evil, arising out of his very nature … He hates evil. His holiness of necessity leads to that.'[20] Similarly, 'sin' was not a 'substance', but was personal and relational: 'You cannot separate sin from persons, so when God deals with sin he has to deal with persons.' In consequence: 'There cannot be a happy relationship between God and man while sin is there. That is precisely what the biblical doctrine of the wrath of God says.'[21]

The cross links these foundational teachings together, revealing the 'holiness of God, the heinousness of sin … the terrible seriousness of man's rebellion against God.'[22] Yet God, in love, found a way whereby 'His own wrath upon sin has its full vent and yet that sinners might be saved.' This act of saving love demonstrates the true character of God, who: 'was declaring publicly once and for ever His eternal justice AND His eternal love. Never separate them, for they belong together in the character of God.'[23]

---

19 D.M. Lloyd-Jones, *Romans: An Exposition of Chapters 3.20–4.25: Atonement and Justification* (Edinburgh: Banner of Truth, 1970), pp. 108, 65–66.

20 Lloyd-Jones, *Romans: An Exposition of Chapters 3.20–4.25,* pp. 75–76.

21 Lloyd-Jones, *Romans: An Exposition of Chapters 3.20–4.25,* pp. 76–77.

22 D.M. Lloyd-Jones, *The Cross: God's Way of Salvation* (Eastbourne: Kingsway, 1986), p. 159.

The love of God was strongly emphasised by Lloyd-Jones. As a medical doctor he delivered his opinion that upon the cross, Jesus literally died of a broken heart. The stream of blood and water seen by the soldiers who pierced his side with a spear was, according to the 'Doctor,' clotted blood and serum, indicating that:

His heart was literally ruptured by the agony of the wrath of God upon him, and by the separation from the face of his Father ... That, my friend, is the love of God to you, a sinner ... And he did it in order that we should not receive that punishment and go to hell ... that is the wonder and the marvel and the glory of the cross ...[24]

The cross reveals that God 'is love and full of mercy and compassion; that God loves us with an everlasting love.'[25]

Lloyd-Jones saw the principle of penal substitution as being written throughout Scripture, from the Old Testament sacrifical system, to Gethsemane, and the cry of dereliction:

If you do not believe in the doctrine of the wrath of God ... what possible meaning is there in that cry of dereliction? What likewise is the meaning of the agony in the Garden? Why did He sweat drops of blood ... Why? Because He knew that He was going to feel the wrath of God against the sin He was to bear, and be separated from His Father.

The penal and substitutionary understanding of the work of Christ is the only explanation for these events:

Our sins have been laid upon Him, and the wrath of God upon those sins has come upon Him ... the punishment that should have come upon you and to me on account of our sinfulness and our sins came to Him.[26]

Here then is the heart of the gospel. Other ways of speaking of the cross in

---

23 Lloyd-Jones, *The Cross: God's Way of Salvation,* pp. 78, 108.

24 Lloyd-Jones, *The Cross,* p. 81.

25 Lloyd-Jones, *The Cross,* p. 183.

26 Lloyd-Jones, *Romans,* pp. 90–91.

Scripture, such as ransom, sacrifice, or reconciliation, only make sense if propitiation lies at their centre. In the cross, all the attributes of God crystallise and operate in absolute harmony: 'The cross not only shows the love of God more gloriously than anything else, it shows his righteousness, His justice, His holiness, and all the glory of His eternal attributes … If you do not see them all, you have not seen the cross.'[27]

J.I. PACKER

One Anglican theologian much influenced by Martyn Lloyd-Jones was James I. Packer. In his 1973 Tyndale Biblical Theology Lecture he bravely took a stand not only against liberals who were rejecting penal substitution as offensive and outdated, but also against some evangelicals who were equivocating on the teaching. He firmly declared his conviction that 'belief that Christ's death on the cross had the character of penal substitution' was a 'distinguishing mark of the worldwide evangelical fraternity,' and takes us 'to the very heart of the Christian gospel.'[28] On the cross:

Jesus expiated our sins, propitiated our Maker, turned God's 'no' to us into a 'yes', and so saved us.[29]

Packer argued that other ways of speaking of the cross, such as victory, or as an example to inspire our love, are important, and he laments as 'perverse' the view that 'accounts of the cross which have appeared as rivals in historical debate must be treated as instrinsically exclusive.' Nonetheless, he sought to defend the 'much disputed claim that a broadly substitutionary view of the cross has always been the mainstream Christian opinion,'[30] and that, although frequently misrepresented, penal substitution was of foundational importance. So he affirmed that:

---

27 Lloyd-Jones, *Romans,* p. 106.

28 J.I. Packer, 'What did the Cross Achieve? The Logic of Penal Substitution', *Tyndale Bulletin,* 25 (1974), reprinted in **J.I. Packer,** *Celebrating the Saving Work of God: The Collected Shorter Writings of J.I. Packer* (Carlisle: Paternoster, 1998), p. 86.

29 Packer, 'What did the Cross Achieve?', p. 101.

'Jesus Christ ... the God-man ... took our place under judgement, and received in his own personal experience all the dimensions of the death that was our sentence ... our sins have already been judged and punished ... in the person and death of another.'

This is the experience of believers, who look at Calvary and affirm that 'Jesus was bearing the judgement I deserved (and deserve), the penalty for my sins, the punishment due to me ... How it was possible for him to bear their penalty they do not claim to know ... but that he bore it is the certainty on which all their hopes rest.'[31] He summed this up very simply elsewhere:

Jesus knew on the cross all the pain, physical and mental, that man could inflict and also the divine wrath and rejection that my sins deserve; for he was there in my place, making atonement for me.[32]

JOHN STOTT

Another significant defence of the atonement as a work of penal substitution came with John Stott's *The Cross of Christ* (1986). The need for the cross is rooted in the holiness of God, who is too pure to look upon evil. Wrath is God's holy reaction to evil. Stott argued that we must not lose sight of 'the biblical revelation of the living God who hates evil, is disgusted and angered by it, and refuses ever to come to terms with it.'[33] Stott recognises that teaching on penal substitution has not only been misrepresented, it has on occasions been inadequately presented by its supporters. God and Christ should not be presented as if they 'acted independently of each other or were in conflict with each other.' Instead

---

30 Packer, 'What did the Cross Achieve?' p. 101.

31 Packer, 'What did the Cross Achieve?', pp. 109–110.

32 J.I. Packer, *I Want to Be A Christian* (Eastbourne: Kingsway, 1985), pp. 45–46. Other noteworthy Anglican defences have included **Leon Morris,** *The Apostolic Preaching of the Cross* (London: Tyndale Press, 1955) and, interestingly, **George Carey** (later to become Archbishop of Canterbury), *The Gate of Glory* (London: Hodder and Stoughton, 1986).

33 J. Stott, *The Cross of Christ* (London: IVP, 1986), pp. 102–03, 109.

they took the 'initiative together to save sinners ... The Father did not lay on the Son an ordeal he was unwilling to bear, nor did the Son extract from the Father a salvation he was reluctant to bestow.' Rather, one should speak of 'God acting in and through Christ with his whole-hearted concurrence.'[34]

The atonement is something that cuts away at human pride and self-sufficiency, which perhaps explains why it is so opposed:

Instead of inflicting upon us the judgement we deserved, God in Christ endured it in our place. Hell is the only alternative. This is a 'scandal', the stumbling block, of the cross. For our proud hearts rebel against it. We cannot bear to acknowledge either the seriousness of our sin and guilt or our utter indebtedness to the cross. Surely, we say, there must be something we can do, or at least contribute, in order to make amends.[35]

The love of God is firmly placed by Stott at the heart of the atonement: 'It cannot be emphasised too strongly that God's love is the source, not the consequence, of the atonement.' Salvation flows from this: 'God does not love us because Christ died for us; Christ died for us because God loved us.' God, who because of his justice, needed to be propitiated, 'took his own loving initiative to appease his own righteous anger by bearing it in His own Son, when he took our place and died for us.' Stott explores the richness of biblical ways of speaking of the atonement, such as redemption, justification and reconciliation, but he concludes that penal substitution is 'the essence of each image and the heart of the atonement itself:' Without it the other images 'could not stand.' He also challenges those who suggest that the substitutionary view of the cross has no moral and social outcome: 'The community of Christ is a community of the cross, and will therefore be marked by sacrifice, service, and suffering.'[36]

---

34 Stott, *The Cross of Christ,* pp. 151, 156.

35 Stott, *The Cross of Christ,* p. 161.

36 Stott, *The Cross of Christ,* pp. 174–75, 203, 289.

BILLY GRAHAM

The dominant figure in American evangelicalism in the second half of the twentieth century was the evangelist Billy Graham. In direct, challenging, and highly charged fashion he preached the gospel to audiences in America, and then world-wide. The series of sermons he preached in his 1958 campaign in Charlotte, North Carolina, are typical of his approach at the time, and contain frequent references to the cross. In the atonement the love of God is supremely demonstrated; it is the only way of salvation, and that upon which the life-changing response of conversion should be based. The seriousness of sin incurs a penalty which only the substitutionary death of Christ can deal with:

He alone had in His body and His soul the capacity to bear sins ... we deserve death and we deserve judgement and we deserve hell. But Jesus said, 'I will take the judgement, I will take the hell, and I will take the suffering' ... Only He could be offered as a sacrifice that would be pleasing to God and would reconcile God and man together.[37]

That this was freely done is emphasised: 'He volunteered to take my judgement. He volunteered to take my sins. He volunteered to take my hell. And Jesus, out of love for us, went to that cross and suffered and bled and died.'[38]

Aware of the impossibility of reducing the atonement to a simple form of words, Billy Graham stressed that at its core it must be seen as penal and substitutionary:

We do not understand it all. You cannot compress the atonement of Christ into one particular theory. There is mystery about it ... it was the judgement of Christ for sin. Now Jesus Christ took the hell, the destruction and judgement at the cross. When you

---

37 W. Graham, 'The Darkest Hour', Sermon Preached at Charlotte crusade, 18 October 1958, transcribed from *Charlotte Observer*, 1 Oct 1958, in Billy Graham Centre Archives, Wheaton College, http://www.wheaton.edu/bgc/archives.

38 W. Graham, 'God's Forgetfulness', Sermon preached at Charlotte crusade on 1 Oct 1958, transcribed from *Charlotte Observer*, 2 Oct 1958, BGC Archives.

come to the cross and receive Christ, God appropriates that death of Christ, the blood of Christ, the righteousness of Christ to you.[39]

The substitutionary death of Christ remained not only at the heart of the preaching of evangelists, it remained a key theme in twentieth-century hymns, as reflected in the words of Charles Gabriel:

He took my sins and my sorrows
He made them his very own
And bore the burden to Calvary,
And suffered and died alone.[40]

THE UNCERTAINTIES OF THE LATE TWENTIETH CENTURY

In many denominations, such as Methodism where it had been so strongly affirmed in the eighteenth century, teaching on penal substitution was fading. Adherence to the Westminster Confession became increasingly notional in the Church of Scotland, although retained with firm conviction by evangelicals in the Kirk, and by the Free Church of Scotland.

In evangelical circles, particularly conservative ones, the teaching remained firmly embedded. It was to prove a distinguishing characteristic of evangelicalism in the face of the rise of theological liberalism. The formation in 1928 of the Inter-Varsity Fellowship of Evangelical Unions (or IVF—renamed the Universities and Colleges Christian Fellowship, or UCCF, in 1974) was a response to the widespread acceptance of liberal theology. It was an alternative to the Student Christian Movement whose leaders rejected so many key evangelical doctrines. In 1927 the SCM General Secretary had declared that, 'The doctrine of the verbal inspiration of the Scriptures is as dead as Queen Anne', and delivered his opinion that 'No theologian worth the name accepts the penal view of the

---

39 W. Graham, 'The Great Judgement', Sermon Preached at Charlotte crusade, 19 Oct 1958, transcribed from *Charlotte Observer*, 20 Oct 1958, BGC Archives.

40 From the hymn of **Charles Gabriel** [1856–1932] 'I stand amazed in the presence.'

atonement.'[41] In contrast, the UCCF statement of faith (based on that of the IVF) affirms Christ as the 'substitute' who deals with the 'penalty' of sin: 'Sinful human beings are redeemed from the guilt, penalty and power of sin only through the sacrificial death once for all time of their representative and substitute, Jesus Christ, the only mediator between them and God.'[42]

The Evangelical Alliance statement of Faith of 1970 described the 'substitutionary sacrifice' of the Son of God, as the 'sole and all-sufficient ground of redemption from the guilt and power of sin, and from its eternal consequences,' [Clause 4] and a 'penal' element is strongly implied by its understanding of the 'universal sinfulness and guilt of fallen man', which makes him 'subject to God's wrath and condemnation' [Clause 3]. Therefore, if Christ has borne sin and its eternal consequences, this must include 'wrath and condemnation', which is what the framers of the statement intended to be conveyed. Similar wording is used in the 2005 revision of this statement.[43]

However, when the Fellowship of Independent Evangelical Churches (FIEC) revised its statement of Faith in the early 1990s, it wisely determined to leave no room for ambiguity: 'The Lord Jesus Christ is fully God and fully man ... On the cross he died in the place of sinners, bearing God's punishment for their sin, redeeming them by his blood.'[44]

For Tom Smail, the one time Director of the Fountain Trust, and a

---

41 D. Johnson, *Contending for the Faith: A History of the Evangelical Movement in the Universities and Colleges* (Leicester: IVP, 1979), pp. 131, 137–39; **G. Fielder,** *Lord of the Years: Sixty Years of Student Witness* (Leicester: IVP, 1988), p. 37.

42 Doctrinal Basis of the UCCF, UCCF, 38 De Montfort Street, Leicester.

43 Evangelical Alliance (UK), *Basis of Faith* (1970). The 2005 revision of the EA statement of faith again refers to the cross in substitutionary terms, as 'the atoning sacrifice of Christ on the cross: dying in our place, paying the price of sin, defeating evil, so reconciling us to God.' [Clause 6] Again, a penal substitutionary position is strongly implied when this is read along with Clause 4, which states that sin 'incurs divine wrath and judgement', although strangely the opportunity to make this explicit was not taken.

44 FIEC Statement of Faith, Clause 4.

leading figure in the charismatic movement, the cross of Christ was 'the point of confrontation of human sin and divine wrath. Both unload themselves on to him.' Through the death of Christ came 'the execution of God's judgement upon the sin of the world.' He not only dealt with the rebellion of humanity by his obedience, he also affirmed the rightness of God's judgement against sin, and bore it. However, whilst speaking of the punishment borne by Christ, Smail noted the danger of placing the judgement of God in unresolved tension with his love, and lamented that often little was said about the free grace of the Father who, out of his 'intense desire for the homecoming of sinners', let his Son go to the cross.[45]

What has been affirmed by evangelicals in doctrinal statements concerning the centrality of the cross, is confirmed by writers of contemporary worship hymns and songs. Graham Kendrick's 1989 song, 'Come and see the King of love', is an example:

Come and weep, come and mourn for your sin that pierced Him there,
So much deeper than the wounds of thorn and nail,
All our pride, all our greed, all our fallenness and shame;
And the Lord has laid the punishment on Him.
    We worship at your feet, where wrath and mercy meet,
    And a guilty world is washed by love's pure stream.[46]

This is how the atoning death of Christ has been understood by Christians across almost two thousand years. It has inspired worship, and devotion to Christ. It has helped Christians explain both the teaching of the Bible and their personal experience of salvation, for almost all of that period. Believers should not lightly discard what has stood such a test of time and experience. For these reasons, and in the face of what many in his denomination were saying, the Methodist minister of Westminster Central Hall in London, Dinsdale Young (1861–1938), took a courageous stand

45 T. Smail, *The Forgotten Father: Rediscovering the Heart of the Christian Gospel* (London: Hodder and Stoughton, 1987), pp. 126–27, 138.

46 G. Kendrick, *Come and See,* © Make Way Music, 1989.

that is a challenge to Christians today. He refused to abandon what was so dear to him:

Every day I live, yes every day, this possesses me more and more completely in mind and heart—that that death was a substitution. I know it is an old-fashioned word, a word that is spurned in some quarters. I confess that it satisfies my guilty conscience and comforts my troubled heart, and gives me joy in my religion incomparable when I look up and say, he took my place. I cannot understand it. But he did it; He bore my sins in His own body on the tree.[47]

---

47 On **Dinsdale Young**'s theology see his *Stars of Retrospect: Frank Chapters of Autobiography* (London: Hodder and Stoughton, 1920). The quotation was kindly supplied by Rev. John Brand of AIM International.

Conclusion

In recent debate over the nature of the atoning work of Christ, it has been suggested that the doctrine of penal substitution belongs particularly to the Reformed tradition, and especially to a line leading from John Calvin, through to Charles Hodge.[1] This appears to be an attempt to marginalise the doctrine into belonging to only one strand within evangelicalism, and to suggest that today's understanding of penal substitution is the historically unrepresentative child of nineteenth-century American Reformed thinking. Certainly the understanding of the atonement as a work of penal substitution has been strongly held by those in the Reformed tradition. However, this survey has shown how the teaching that Christ acting as the substitute for sinners and bearing the penalty due for their sin—the righteous punishment that comes from a just and holy God—has been held by Christians in every period in the history of the church.

The terminology has sometimes varied—many early church thinkers emphasised the word 'curse' rather than penalty—but the meaning has remained substantially the same. Other ways of speaking about the atonement have certainly also been used in the history of the church, reflecting the rich range of teaching in the Scriptures, but alongside, and in absolute harmony with these, the understanding that the death of Christ was both penal and substitutionary has been understood as lying at the heart of the biblical teaching. The issue was not one of significant conflict during the Reformation, and both Protestants and Catholics agreed that the death of Christ was a work of propitiation, although between these two groupings there remained very significant differences over understanding how the work of the cross was applied to the sinner. For many centuries only those who stood outside of Christian orthodoxy significantly diverged from this pattern of understanding. Indeed, it was not until the

---

1 E.g. **J.B. Green and M.D. Baker**, *Rediscovering the Scandal of the Cross* (Carlisle: Paternoster, 2003), esp. pp. 142–150; **S. Chalke,** 'Cross Purposes', *Christianity and Renewal*, Sept. 2004, pp. 44–48.

nineteenth century that voices within mainstream Protestantism began to adopt liberal theological views that had previously been rejected as unorthodox.

Within evangelicalism, as a leading historian has succinctly expressed it:

Belief that Christ died in our stead was not uniform in the Evangelical tradition, but it was normal ... What Evangelicals agreed on seemed of infinitely greater importance than their disagreements, and their pre-eminent ground of agreement was the cruciality of the cross.[2]

To Luther it was 'the chief doctrine of the Christian faith', to John Wesley 'the inmost mystery of the Christian faith', and to Spurgeon 'the first, the grandest, the highest, the most essential truth'. Martyn Lloyd-Jones believed it was 'absolutely crucial for a true understanding of Christian doctrine and the way of salvation', and to J.I. Packer it was the 'distinguishing mark of the worldwide evangelical fraternity.' Alister McGrath has called Packer's defence of penal substitution 'classic evangelical orthodoxy.'[3] The belief that the atoning death of Christ was a work of penal substitution remains the 'normal' position of evangelicalism. Viewing penal substitution as just one option amongst a range of ways of thinking of the atonement, which could be either accepted or not, was decisively rejected by leaders such as John Wesley. He asserted that to deny this truth was to 'deny the Lord that bought them.'[4]

---

2 D. Bebbington, *Evangelicalism in Modern Britain* (London: Unwin Hyman, 1989), pp. 16–17.

3 A. McGrath, *To Know and Serve God: A Life of James I. Packer* (London: Hodder and Stoughton, 1997), p. 209. Of around 100 participants at an Evangelical Alliance Symposium on the Atonement in July 2005, 94% still affirmed their belief in a penal substitutionary view of the atonement, although 34% regarded it as only one model among several. Joint Evangelical Alliance-London School of Theology Atonement Symposium, 6–8 July: A Statement by the Evangelical Alliance,
http://www.eauk.org/contentmanager/content/press/statements, accessed 25 October 2005.

4 J. Wesley, *Letters of John Wesley,* Vol. III (London: Epworth, 1931), p. 109. Letter to Dr John Robertson, 24 September 1753.

Conclusion

The penal substitutionary death of Christ is a topic of great mystery, and a matter for profound worship. Statements of the atonement should never become narrowly analytical, or formulaic, but should always become an expression of faith, and a foundation for a life of devotion and self-sacrifice. The difficulty of comprehending, let alone expressing in human words, the glory of the cross, has taxed theologians and preachers through the centuries. How can we convey the meaning of the Trinity, let alone the work of God in and through the atonement? Yet the church has consistently used the language of penal substitution to explain what the Scripture reveals about the transcendent, divine reality of the atonement. Other ways of speaking of the cross are important, but ultimately they only make sense when the substitutionary death of Christ stands at the core.

Because Christ is our substitute, sin and guilt are dealt with, the holy demands of the justice of God are met, God's wrath is propitiated (turned away), and the powers of darkness are overthrown. The glory of this work of substitution, which Luther termed the 'wonderful exchange',[5] has thrilled Christians through the centuries.

It may be fairly argued that the term 'penal substitution' is not found in Scripture, but neither is the word 'Trinity'. A simpler way of expressing the depth of Scripture teaching on this subject does not appear to have been found. The solemn fact remains, as John Owen explained, 'If he fulfilled not justice, I must; if he underwent not wrath, I must to eternity.'[6] Through the centuries, the awesome teaching of penal substitution brought great blessing to troubled souls, and lovingly, wisely, and reverentially preached today, evangelicals can have every confidence that it will continue to do the same.

The need to defend these truths has long been recognised. Being so fundamental, they are bound to be a prime target for spiritual opposition. As Martyn Lloyd-Jones explained, 'What a salvation! Is it surprising that the enemy with all his ingenuity and malignity masses his attack upon this,

---

5 **M. Luther,** *Works of Martin Luther* (Weimar Edition, Weimar: 1883), Vol 5, p. 608.

6 **J. Owen,** 'The Death of Death in the Death of Christ', in *Works of John Owen* (London: Banner of Truth, 1968), Vol X. p. 284.

and would rob these glorious terms of their real and profound meaning?'[7] We live in times when this defence is both necessary and difficult. In the modern West, principles that are foundational to Christians are not only derided, but have been deemed inadmissible. Our age echoes the words of the Hindu speaker who declared in 1893: 'Ye are children of God; the sharers of immortal bliss, holy and perfect beings. It is a sin to call a man a sinner. It is a standing libel on human nature.'[8] A similar reaction is made to the concept of the wrath of God. But in this, perhaps the modern, or post-modern, mind is not so modern after all, for in the second century Marcion only wanted to speak of a God of love, and Greek philosophers decided that wrath was a notion unworthy of being attributed to a deity. The gospel writers did not seek to accommodate their message to account for what was considered unpalatable for their age—whether it was the offence of the cursed cross to Jews, or a holy and sin-judging God to Greeks. Sadly, there have been times when external pressures have unhelpfully shaped what Christians have believed in this area.

History also shows that evangelical Christians have not always expressed the truth of the atonement with sufficient care. Therefore, the last few pages of this book are devoted to a series of eight lessons for Christian belief, preaching, and proclamation about the atonement, which flow from our biblical and historical study.

First, it is important always to stress that the initiative in the atonement lies with God, who in love planned the way of salvation. We must not forget to affirm, 'God so loved the world that ...' From eternity, God in love determined the way of salvation for sinners, by which his justice would be satisfied, and mercy shown.

Secondly, the cross must be preached in a Trinitarian way, recognising always the eternal harmony within the persons of the Godhead. At times the Father has been portrayed as a reluctant player in the act of forgiveness.

---

7 **D.M. Lloyd-Jones,** *Romans: An Exposition of Chapters 3.20–4.25: Atonement and Justification* (Edinburgh: Banner of Truth, 1970), p. 94.

8 **Swami Vivekananda,** at Parliament of Religions in Chicago, in *Speeches and Writings*, pp. 38–39, quoted in **Stott,** *Cross of Christ*, p. 162.

Conclusion

Martyn Lloyd-Jones warned about this: 'We are not teaching that the Lord Jesus Christ has changed the mind of God ... there have been certain zealous evangelical teachers who have said that. But they should never have said so ... Paul does not teach that the Lord Jesus Christ by dying has persuaded God to forgive us ...'[9] According to Sinclair Ferguson, if any hint is given that the Father is the hostile party in the work of the atonement, it will 'poison the Christian's sense of pardon, stability and joy, which are grounded in the knowledge that Christ is truly and fully the revelation of the Father'.[10] The impression of any form of disjunction between the Father and the Son must be strictly avoided: it must not be implied that the Father was unwilling to suffer, nor that Christ was a victim. Nor should he be presented as dying to placate or pacify a Father who is filled with vengeance which was only averted at the last moment by the interception of the Son. Father, Son, and Holy Spirit were at one in their loving eternal plan and purpose, and in its outworking upon the cross. All that the Son did, he did voluntarily and in love.[11]

Thirdly, the wrath of God is a clear biblical teaching, but one which needs to be spoken of with care. This is not the uncontrolled rage of the tyrant, nor the anger of the ogre. God's wrath is pure and undefiled. Sin is hateful to God, it is an offence to his holy presence, and because God is just, sin cannot simply be forgiven, the righteous penalty against it must be served. The

---

9 **Lloyd-Jones,** *Romans*, p. 79.

10 **S. Ferguson,** 'Preaching the Atonement', in **eds. C.E. Hill and F.A. James III,** *The Glory of the Atonement* (Downers Grove, Illinois: IVP, 2004), p. 431.

11 In today's culture, where we have become all too tragically aware of the reality of violent cruelty against children, the language of God striking his Son with his rod in anger, found in some older hymns, perhaps no longer appears appropriate and may be best avoided. Some have claimed that penal substitution legitimates the abuse of children, but this is a perverse distortion of what has been proclaimed down the centuries. The Son was not a child, and the role of suffering was willingly and voluntarily undertaken by the incarnate second person of the Trinity. What he suffered was not as a result of a fit of temper, but of holy and righteous justice, worked out in holy and righteous wrath. Through all, the Son remained the focus of the Father's love.

wrath of God is the outworking of his holiness and justice against sin. But the cross is the supreme demonstration of the love of God—it is the place where wrath and mercy meet. As the Free Kirk theologian John 'Rabbi' Duncan explained it to his students: 'It was *damnation*: and he took it *lovingly*.'[12] The justice and mercy of God should not be set in opposition to each other, one aspect of his character did not prevail over another, but all his attributes were, and remain, in eternal harmony.

Fourthly, the suffering of the cross must be spoken of in all its dimensions. To some, preaching the cross is simply recounting the physical sufferings of Christ, as if that conveyed all that there is to say about Christ. The mental and spiritual tortures of the holy, sinless, Son of God bearing sin and guilt and its punishment were as great, if not greater, than the physical pain—as Gethsemane shows. Linked to this is a tendency to say too little about Christ's life of teaching, healing, and loving care. These were no mere appendages to the cross, but an integral part of his atoning work. Theologians affirm the active obedience of Christ in his incarnate life, fulfilling the law, alongside the passive obedience in and through the cross. The cross comes as the culmination of a life of servanthood and voluntary self-sacrifice, and the totality of the work of the atonement should be emphasised.

A fifth issue is the importance of speaking of both the cross and the resurrection together. Some sermons on Calvary end with a crucifix, not an empty cross. The triumph on the third day should not be separated from the passion narratives, but be seen as an essential part of the work of the atonement. We know assuredly that sin and death are defeated, that the debt has been paid, justice satisfied, and punishment served, because on the third day Christ rose from the dead, and is alive for evermore. Through the resurrection Christ became a life-giving spirit (1 Corinthians 15:45). The resurrection is an integral part of the gospel of a living, vindicated Saviour, who has conquered sin, and death and its rightful punishment. It is fundamental to spiritual new-birth and to the believer's ongoing in the Spirit-filled fellowship with the risen Christ.

---

12 J. Duncan, quoted in **Packer,** 'What did the Cross Achieve?' p. 120.

Conclusion

Sixthly, the richness of biblical ways of speaking of the cross must not be ignored. The Scriptures do speak of the death of Christ using a range of terms such as ransom, reconciliation, participation, redemption, victory, and these must not be ignored. The historical evidence shows how Christians have sought to be faithful to this range of ideas found within the word of God. However, such proclamation will inevitably lead to supplementary questions such as: Why was Christ victorious? How is it that we are reconciled? This will lead us to speak of Christ's substitutionary death as the propitiatory sacrifice, which lies at the heart of all other scriptural ways of speaking of the atonement.

A seventh need is to root the reality of salvation in what God in Christ has done. Martin Luther stressed the importance of the words 'for us', and so must we. Salvation does not rest on a decision a person has made, or an experience they had, it rests on the perfect and finished work of Christ, through his life, death, and resurrection, and the application of that work to us by grace. We should not proclaim the fruits of Christ's work without first preaching Christ, the root of the blessings.

A final need is to show the moral and practical consequences of the atonement for the believer. The fruit of the cross is a new creation. By God's saving grace, believers become new creations, and should live as such. A person is not saved simply by being moved by the example of Christ, but once saved, the example of Christ in the cross should be the inspiration for a profoundly changed way of living. Seeing the atonement as a work of penal substitution should be the most powerful inspiration to love and worship God, and to serve him. If Christ has truly borne our sins, and the punishment due for them, we are free indeed, now and for eternity! How then shall we respond to such a great salvation? Is any sacrifice too great, or any work of service too hard?

Scripture index

Scripture index

General index

General index

AUTHORS

Dr Ian J. Shaw has been Lecturer in Church History at the International Christian College, Glasgow, since 1996. Before this he was the pastor of an Independent Evangelical Church in Manchester. He has a PhD in Church History from the University of Manchester, and is the author of a number of books and articles about issues in the history of evangelicalism.

Brian H. Edwards is the author of fifteen books including two historical biographies and a major study on the inspiration, authority and history of the Bible. He was the pastor of Hook Evangelical Church in Surbiton, Surrey, for nearly thirty years before taking up his present role of preaching, lecturing and writing. Brian's degree in theology was awarded by the University of London.

Ian and Brian have performed a very valuable service for the church at this time. I admire the spirit in which they carefully and faithfully present both the doctrine of the atonement and the history of this belief in the church. It is a vital contribution to recent controversies. The eight lessons presented in the final pages are a model of how we should understand and proclaim this doctrine so central to our faith.

PETER MAIDEN, INTERNATIONAL DIRECTOR OF OPERATION MOBILISATION; CHAIRMAN OF THE KESWICK CONVENTION

Here is a timely reminder, both from a biblical as well as an historical perspective, that the theme of penal substitution has always been at the very heart of biblical Christianity. In a day when so many biblical truths are being undermined, the authors have done an invaluable service to the world church by restating, in balanced and heart-warming ways, what ought to be a non-negotiable truth.

REV. JOHN D. BRAND, UK DIRECTOR, AFRICA INLAND MISSION INTERNATIONAL